What peop

Polytheist

Voices from Pagan Cloisters

Polytheistic Monasticism is a rich and multifaceted introduction to a growing movement with the pagan community. Of particular interest to the druid community are useful accounts of how individual druids have maintained intentional monastic practices and devotionals in spite of the demands of modern life. Through personal accounts, philosophies, and practices, this work offers much insight for readers with an interest in building their own monastic practice. *Polytheistic Monasticism* gives voice to a powerful way of living, being, and communing with the spirits of nature and the divine.

Dana O'Driscoll, Grand Archdruid, AODA & Bishop, Gnostic Celtic Church

This defining and much-needed book fills a void in the polytheist community by giving voice to the small number of monastics who tend the sacred heart of devotion to the gods and spirits, and live disciplined lives of prayer, contemplation, study, and work in accordance with monastic principles. To those called to polytheist monasticism, those who are curious, and those who never knew it existed or was possible, it provides a sound introduction, with well-written illustrations of personal paths.

Lorna Smithers, Brythonic polytheist, author at Gods & Radicals Press

The essays which comprise *Polytheistic Monasticism* are heart-felt, lyrical, and insightful. While the contributors to this anthology have each found their own way to monasticism, and are developing their own practices, their commitment to their calling is soul deep. As monastics, they strive for divine union; through prayer and work, they seek to become a meeting place between the spirit world and human world, to cultivate both inner and outer sacred space. Their creativity, devotion, discipline, and dedication are an inspiration to polytheists everywhere.

Rebecca Buchanan, editor of *Eternal Haunted Summer*

This book deepens our understanding of the Western polytheistic revival, bringing to light devotional and ethical aspects neglected in popular accounts of the movement, but which represent increasingly important dynamics within it. An essential contribution for researchers following developments in this field.

Edward P. Butler, PhD, Director, Center for Global Polytheist and Indigenous Traditions, Indic Academy

This is one of those books that fills a deep need in the Pagan and Polytheist communities, one that many may not even have fully realized was there. By offering tools and ideas for creating a focused path of contemplation and devotion, the many and varied writers are providing the sort of advanced material that is very often called for but seldom fully delivered. And while there are frequent nods to the ubiquity of monotheism in modern discussions of monasticism, *Polytheistic Monasticism* avoids being just another monotheistic text wrapped in polytheistic clothing, instead giving ways to create something that serves our communities' unique needs.

Lupa, author of *Nature Spirituality From the Ground Up* and *The Tarot of Bones*

Polytheistic Monasticism is a warm, full-souled exploration of modern Western polytheist monasticism that invites the reader into each cloister with a warm fire and nourishing food. It offers an expanded understanding of what is possible for modern Pagans and polytheists.

Sarenth Odinsson, Heathen spiritworker, author of *Calling to Our Ancestors*

This is an inspiring and interesting read! If you are drawn to the solitary life, then this is a must. However, even if the monastic life is not for you, this is still well worth a read, full of a wisdom that can be applied to every life journey.

Philip Carr-Gomm, author of *Druid Mysteries*, and *Seek Teachings Everywhere*

Polytheistic Monasticism

Voices from Pagan Cloisters

Polytheistic Monasticism

Voices from Pagan Cloisters

Edited by Janet Munin

MOON
BOOKS

Winchester, UK
Washington, USA

JOHN HUNT PUBLISHING

First published by Moon Books, 2022
Moon Books is an imprint of John Hunt Publishing Ltd., No. 3 East Street, Alresford
Hampshire SO24 9EE, UK
office@jhpbooks.net
www.johnhuntpublishing.com
www.moon-books.net

For distributor details and how to order please visit the 'Ordering' section on our website.

Text copyright: Janet Munin 2021

ISBN: 978 1 78904 891 9
978 1 78904 892 6 (ebook)
Library of Congress Control Number: 2021934864

A CIP catalogue record for this book is available from the British Library.

Design: Stuart Davies

UK: Printed and bound by CPI Group (UK) Ltd, Croydon, CR0 4YY
Printed in North America by CPI GPS partners

We operate a distinctive and ethical publishing philosophy in
all areas of our business, from our global network of authors to
production and worldwide distribution.

Contents

Also edited by Janet Munin

Queen of the Great Below: An Anthology in Honor of Ereshkigal
ISBN: 978-1453878965

Polytheism: The worship of more than one deity or holy power. Polytheism is not synonymous with Paganism. Not all pagans believe in more than one deity (some do not believe in any deity at all) and not all polytheists identify as pagans. Polytheism exists in varied forms throughout the world, and has for millennia. In the context of this volume, "modern polytheists" or simply "polytheists" will refer only to those practicing within the very wide context of the Polytheistic Revival in modern Western culture. The editor and contributors acknowledge and honor the polytheists of other faiths whose practices have endured for centuries and continue to thrive in the modern era.

Introduction

Janet Munin

The religions of the world are diverse and complex, but there are some roles which are recognizable across time, culture, language, and tradition. Among these are:

- Ritual priests, who perform the rites which maintain the contracts and connections between humanity and the Holy Powers, and hold the forces of chaos at bay.
- Shepherd-pastors, who tend to the needs of the laity/ community.
- Teachers, who preserve, elaborate on, and pass down sacred stories and protocols.
- Diviners, who discern and interpret the will of the Holy Powers and the lessons of fate.
- Healers, who mediate the power of the Divine to promote health and wholeness.

Not all of these roles are represented in every tradition, and often a single person or office will encompass more than one, but again and again throughout the world and down through the millennia we see these functions carried out. They express the fundamental purposes of religion and the needs of humanity seeking ongoing relationship with the Holy Powers.

These roles are found within the modern Western Polytheist Revival, performed by holders of various official titles as well as those with no title at all. Even though many within this very broad umbrella reject what they consider "conventional religion" these roles still emerge as individuals and groups develop their own traditions.

The sixth recurring religious role is that of the monastic. It is far less common than the first five, but still recognizable across cultures. Monastics are those who take solemn vows to live centered on their relationship with one or more Holy Power. Anything which impedes or compromises that relationship is left behind or minimized as much as possible. They are renunciates, offering up wealth, social status, a conventional career, and family life on the altar of devotion. Monasticism usually involves living in a community under the authority of a religious superior and the Rule of the Order. The Rule is the defining document of an Order, describing the purpose of the community, the ritual schedule, the leadership roles, and how community members are to behave at any given time.

Some monastically-inclined individuals live alone, as hermits. Like those in community, a hermit embraces simplicity for the sake of ever-deepening focus on the object(s) of their worship and devotion. If they are part of a religion which has a monastic element, they may need to seek formal approval and support to pursue a solitary monastic life, or they may unofficially choose to do so because they do not wish to join a community. A person drawn to monasticism within a religion which does not have a monastic element may become a hermit because they have no other option.

The contributors to this volume live as hermits, either because they are part of a religious tradition which does not have a monastic element, because they comprise a "tradition of one," or because their monastic Order does not have religious communities. All of them are part of the Pagan-Polytheist Revival, a movement popularly characterized as earthy, sensual, rebellious, individualistic, and ecstatic– a surprising context in which to pursue a path of renunciation. Even other polytheists whose practices are not characterized by the above qualities are often surprised to learn that there are monastics among them.

Creating Modern Polytheistic Monasticism

Catholics, Episcopalians, Hindus, and Buddhists who are called to monasticism have centuries-old traditions to support, nurture, and guide them. They step into a long line of those who have sworn the same vows, adopted the same garb, lived within the same walls, and conformed their lives to the same Rule. Modern polytheists seeking monastic life do not have centuries of tradition or extensive institutional support to define their path or support them on it. They do not even find a place within the New Monasticism[1] movement which, while ecumenical, remains firmly monotheistic and thus in many ways incompatible with polytheistic cosmologies and values. But even without an authoritative definition, those who embrace the title of polytheistic monastic and who have shared their practices in this volume reveal several common characteristics.

The monastic's life is focused on devotion to one or more Holy Powers, usually formalized with vows. Because of this focus, the monastic practices some degree of asceticism, removing distractions to spiritual life which are taken for granted by others: wealth acquisition, social life, media consumption, etc.

The monastic lives according to a Rule or other structure which supports and reinforces their vowed life. Some of these are formal, breaking each day and season down into a deliberate, repetitive order. Contemplation, prayer, study, worship, chores, rest, and recreation all have a place and are engaged in deliberately, at the appropriate time. Others are less formal and detailed, but still serve as a mindful framework for the monastic's daily life.

Strikingly absent from this list is the triple vow of "Poverty, chastity and obedience."[2] Those renunciations were developed within large faith communities, most of which denigrated life in the world and the comfort of the body in favor of a "higher" spiritual existence. Modern polytheists bring very different sensibilities to these areas.

Traditional monastic poverty requires that each individual have little or no personal possessions. Any assets they enjoyed as a layperson are given away or donated to the monastery when they enter. In return, the monastery and the institution supporting it guarantees the monk or nun shelter, food, and other basic necessities of life. Mendicant orders take the vow of poverty even farther, living only on alms and other donations. Western polytheistic monastics do not have the support of an institution providing for their material needs, nor do they live within a culture that encourages the practice of giving alms to mendicants. As noted above, most of the contributors to this book practice some degree of asceticism, but none feel compelled to live in poverty. Some, such as Syren Nagakyrie[3], turn the question of voluntary poverty on its head and use their monasticism as a lens through which they criticize the capitalist system that leaves so many people suffering involuntary poverty.

Obedience is another requirement based on community and institutional living. A novice monastic swears to obey his or her superiors in their order and to obey the Rule. Monastic polytheists have no superiors except the Holy Powers. Even those who are part of a formal Order cannot be compelled to obedience by the leaders or punished for lack of compliance with the Rule, although they may lose their right to be affiliated with the group if they stray too far beyond the boundaries which define it.

And chastity? Modern Neo-Paganism and animism are famous – if not infamous – for embracing the goodness of the natural world, including the body and senses. Adherents seldom find spiritual value in denying sexuality.[4] None of the monastics in this volume write about being called to chastity, but very few have partners. It may be that the ability to live without a human partner is a characteristic of the psycho-spiritual character of those called to monasticism.

Monastics Without Monasteries

Not only do most of these contributors not have romantic partnerships, all of them live outside the support of a vowed community. As noted above, monasticism in general practice refers to a community-based lifestyle. The community supports and reinforces the Rule all are sworn to, and each individual contributes to the work which supports the whole: cooking, cleaning, gardening, mending, bookkeeping, and the myriad other chores which must be done to support life in the material world. The community also serves as a spiritual crucible, challenging the members to maintain the values and ideals of their path while living at close quarters with other flawed human beings.

Some polytheistic monastics are content to live as hermits, but others yearn for the ability to build and live in a monastic community. Unfortunately, the challenges to this are many, and the most basic is the diversity inherent in the term "polytheistic." Classically, a monastic community is based on a common theology and a single Rule to which all must adhere. It's virtually impossible to find such unity of belief and practice even in "denominations" such as Druids, Heathens, and Wiccans, or even the few established Orders within those communities. How does a group of monastically-inclined individuals formulate a meaningful Rule for a community if the members have been called to different practices and vows? How will the community be defined and regulated to the benefit of all, including the various Holy Powers represented? It is a challenge yet to be surmounted on a large scale.

Even if a group of polytheistic monastics could agree on a Rule, there would remain the challenge of finding a place to establish a community. Buying or building the property necessary for community life, and then maintaining it in good condition, is a financial challenge which has been overcome by only one Order.[5]

Like thousands of others who find themselves isolated from those who share their interests or beliefs, polytheistic monastics use the internet to connect with others on the same path. Through social media, personal websites, and email, they share resources, experiences, and mutual encouragement.

Individual Paths

The authors in this anthology represent a wide range of religious affiliations, degrees of complexity of Rule, and types of spiritual practices. Some essays are very personal accounts of developing a Rule or discovering a calling. Others address more general topics about monasticism or monastic practices. Every author but one explicitly identifies as a monastic.

The exception is John Michael Greer, a founder of the Gnostic Celtic Church. His book about the Order's beliefs and practices[6] includes a discussion of "the Hermitage of the Heart," a concept which has been cited by many as inspiration for their exploration of monasticism.[7] Because no other resource was mentioned as frequently, I reached out to Greer to invite him to contribute an expanded discussion of the topic for this book, and he graciously agreed.

These writers are weaving something both ancient and new into the living traditions of modern polytheism. I invite you to explore their paths of discipline and devotion.

Endnotes

1   See *New Monasticism: An Interspiritual Manifesto for Contemplative Living*, by Rory McEntee and Adam Bucko. ORBIS. 2015.

2   There are polytheists who engage in chastity as part of their spiritual practices, but it is not a definitive element of polytheistic monasticism.

3   See "Modern Polytheistic Monasticism: A Revolutionary Vision" in this volume.

4   Neo-Pagan sexual ethics tend to center around issues of consent, honesty, and protecting the vulnerable.

5   The Matreum of Cybele in Palenville, New York.

6   *The Gnostic Celtic Church: A Manual and Book of Liturgy*, by John Michael Greer. Starseed Publishing. 2013.

7   "The Hermitage of the Heart" was mentioned frequently by participants in the Forum of Polytheistic Monastics.

Chapter 1

Finding Monasticism

Aine Llewellyn

I wasn't raised in an especially religious household; at most, it could be described as loosely Pagan. Yet I've been drawn to the Gods and monastic practice as long as I can remember. My areligious nonreligious background meant I had little knowledge of the path that was calling me. All that I knew was the longing in my heart.

When I did finally learn about monasticism, I was well-enmeshed within Pagan and polytheist practice. I had begun teaching myself about modern Paganism (largely Wicca) since I was twelve and stumbled upon Wiccan texts. At the time, I was operating from an eclectic Wiccan-esque framework, one that hardly seemed to align with monastic impulses or practices. Not to mention that I was solidly a polytheist and suspected I would remain so. My exposure to monastic groups was that they were almost, if not entirely, monotheistic. As much as the trappings of abbeys and monasteries appealed to me, I could not envision myself turning away from the multitude of Gods I worshiped to join one.

The Paganism I was reading about at the time never even touched on monasticism. Daily devotional practices were infrequent topics until I moved away from the popular and easily accessible Wiccan-witchcraft books to more reconstructionist and revivalist[1] texts. These better suited what I had been trying to explore within a Wiccan-esque paradigm, but monasticism still seemed an impossibility. Modern Paganism and polytheism were so small and fragmented that support for a monastic community would be difficult to muster. I wasn't aware at the time of the various types of monasticism, such as those nuns who live on their own or outside of monasteries in apartments. I dismissed my passion for devotion. Even when experiencing visceral yearning for the Gods and a life arranged around them, I didn't think of it as a monastic calling. Maybe it would have been possible if I had been raised Christian, I thought, ironically frustrated at my solidly not-monotheistic upbringing.

When I did learn of polytheist monastics my heart fluttered with excitement and my mind burned with renewed hope. Except I found myself assuming that what they were doing was fundamentally different - and fundamentally better - than anything I could. I thought this even when I was spending every waking moment praying and contemplating and creating for my Gods, orienting my life so thoroughly around Them that anyone else would have been hard-pressed to not identify me as some sort of nun.

I convinced myself that most polytheists did just as much, if not more, than I - and that monastics had some inherent quality that made them nuns or monks or wed to the Gods. Vows or oaths or the actual practices didn't factor in. Surely, the vicious voice inside me said, it was simply that they possessed some special innate trait that allowed them to attain what I craved. My hyper-focus on modern Paganism had resulted in my ignorance of the variety and breadth of monastic living in traditions actively practicing it. I had turned monasticism into a caricature of itself in my mind.

This only changed when I took a step back from religion (my own specific tradition and Paganism as a whole). I never stopped entirely, as the Gods were never far from my mind or heart, but I allowed myself to go fallow. I gave myself permission to contemplate without forcing my mind one way or another. I let myself take a break from prayer and devotion. I looked into other religious traditions and explored more widely than before.

I wasn't sure what would happen in that time. Maybe I would discover I preferred a life not dedicated to the Gods. Maybe the calling had calmed once I reached adulthood. Perhaps it had been driven less by Gods and more by teenage hormones, as was often implied by my family when I dared to express my devotional life. Or maybe the Gods would call me again.

In that fallow time, where I wandered in the dark purposefully, my passion for devotion returned to me. I desired prayer. I longed for the structure I had been building in my life. I felt, again, the call of the Gods. I grasped the important truth that what separated me from the polytheist nuns and monks I was reading about was not some inherent quality I lacked but my own ignorance and mental blocks, ones built by society and by my insecurity.

My monastic practice still isn't exactly where I want it to be. I'm discovering it alongside my Gods, after all. I'm finding my Rule of Life. And Gods know I'm struggling with mealtime prayers. Arranging my life around the Holy Ones is most natural for me, though, after doing so for so long (without even realizing what, exactly, I was doing). My devotion, my solitude, and my contemplation are all consciously chosen ways to build this new monasticism.

My resting period allowed me to find my way back to this path. The period of trial and discovery let me return with my eyes clearer, my mind tempered, and my heart opened to what I had been pursuing the whole time.

Endnote

1   Reconstructionists attempt to re-create the earliest-known practices of a religion. Revivalists consider past practices an inspiration but do not seek to duplicate them. (ed)

Chapter 2

Called by the Spirits, but not to the Priesthood

Kimberly Kirner

Portions of this chapter were originally published in "The Wild Druid," a blog on the Pagan Bloggers site.

There is a deep knowing, in my own experience, when a spirit calls you and claims you. I felt that I could run away, but regardless of how long I ran, They had infinite patience and devotion in Their pursuit. I knew that I belonged to Them, and They belonged to me, in a way that is difficult to explain and not always comfortable – but is integral to our mutual development and spiritual work in the world. I imagine that others, most often called by gods, but some called by nature spirits, or ancestors, or fae, experience something similar if they are called. But called to do what? We may be called, but not to the priesthood.

In contemporary Paganism or polytheism, this can be confusing. There are few visible roles in most neo-Pagan communities. The primary role that we see is the priest: the ritualist, the organizer, the "Big Name Pagan" who authors books and blog posts, the workshop presenter. Priests are public figures. They facilitate spiritual and religious experiences for other people. Their responsibilities, training, and authority vary by religious tradition in the world, but what unites priests cross-religiously is their simultaneous service to spirits and to a human community.

But what if we are called not to be priests, but monks or nuns? What if we are called by spirits, but not to public religious leadership? What if our spiritual work in the world is inward-facing, not outward-facing? What is this Spirit-Led Work?

The Spirits I Serve called me to specific purposes in this life, but none of them involve priestly duties. Some of my soul's purpose (and its work with Them) is embedded in my professional work, because the Spirits I Serve are interested in human development and do not care if that development is directed toward Them. Some of the purpose is found in contemplative, solitary practice – it is the work of self-transformation and holding a center, an essence, of divine connection in the world. I'm not alone in this calling; there are people called to this type of practice from many religious traditions in the world and diverse Pagan and polytheist orientations.

Pagan and Polytheist Monasticism

Monasticism is conventionally thought of as a religious path in which monks and nuns renounce worldly pursuits in order to pursue a deeply spiritual life, usually involving long periods of silence, devotional work, contemplative prayer or meditation, and embodied activity in nature (through mindful walking, farming, or simple chores). For most Pagan and polytheist monastics, like some monks and nuns, we do not fully renounce worldly pursuits. This is impossible without strong economic support from a larger community of householders engaged in the world. But in addition to this logistical problem, many monks and nuns (even in religions that offer full renunciation of the world) select to engage more deeply with the world than the average person, balancing this with long periods of contemplation and devotion. There are Buddhist monasteries that run rural schools and development organizations and Catholic monks and nuns who march all over the world to bring awareness to the need for demilitarization and peace. There are those who are doctors, nurses, aid workers, and teachers. The critical pieces of monasticism, at least in how I have come to define it, are devotion, discipline, and contemplation.

Devotion

Monastics, like many priests, share in an often-fierce devotion to the spirit(s) who called them. This might be a god or pantheon, nature spirits and forces, fae, or ancestors. The difference is that their devotion is usually inward-oriented. The demand the spirit makes of the monastic is to give their life to deepening a relationship, not necessarily aiding others directly in connecting to that spirit. Rather than a life of organizing and writing rituals, teaching workshops, and writing books, the monastic has a foundation that involves long periods of what appears to the outside world as doing nothing. It is in the not-doing that the monastic can enter a state of being, of union, rather than a state of action. This does not mean that a monastic cannot lead ritual or that their services are never open to the public. But that is not the main function of the monastic's spiritual life.

We might think of the monastic's primary purpose as one of the developments of divine union, a maintenance of a spiritual "place" of connection between the spirit world and the human world, a cultivation of a constancy in this union. The monastic serves as an essence of the meeting point between divinity and humanity, usually stripped to its simplest form. This is why, in part, monastics in many traditions wear a simple garment, practice in permanent sanctuaries, and maintain a strong but simple rhythm to their lives. The simplicity cuts out the noise of the world; the rhythm of the monastic life builds a strong foundation for consistent connection to the divine.

My greatest desire and most consistent pursuit since I was very young has been in cultivating a life of devotion to the divine – and in my case, particularly as a mystic. Seeking a sense of direct union, a feeling of losing my more tangible but impermanent parts of myself in connecting to the Spirits I Serve, gives me an inexplicable joy and peace – even as it also does not come easily. Maintaining a religious rhythm is very difficult for me, and I would imagine it is so for many aspiring Pagan and polytheist monastics. Our overculture in the United States is inherently less than compatible with a monastic life. Even when we are able to sacrifice some of the clutter of mainstream life, most of us find it necessary to work a wage job, and with it comes all of life's complexities and their tendency to derail the monastic rhythm. I think what defines the monastic heart, however, is a deep and lasting longing for and calling to reestablishing such a rhythm again and again. Devotion is not about perfect action, but rather constancy of effort. Whether in community or hermitage, this effort is bent toward deepening the individual monastic's openness to the spirit(s) they serve. The way I describe this is that though I work a job and am married, my entire orientation in life is through devotion first to the Spirits I Serve. My job must be in alignment with values that are connected to Their own. My marriage must support and uphold mutual spiritual development as a foundation. My life is my offering to Them.

Priests, too, may feel this sense of devotion to the spirits they serve. However, it is likely that their expression of this devotion differs. The priest serves the spirits through serving their community; the monastic finds community (if they are not in hermitage) through serving the spirits. The focal point for their respective efforts differs. In other traditions, when monastics lead ritual, it is typically through letting the public in, not in disrupting the monastic rhythm. This is unlike the priest's function, which is primarily to serve a public religious community, and therefore to generate rituals, services, events, and teachings that resonate with a broad public. I dream that one day, there will be animist and polytheist temples that serve a diverse public. But I am not called to create or maintain those places or the services that would happen in them. Instead, I feel called to create and maintain my own little sanctuary: my shrine room, my gardens. I hope one day to offer a little guest cabin to those who need retreat into silence, into the darkness of the night sky and the beauty of surrounding mountains. I want to offer hospitality, but through opening windows of time and space for others to do their own deeper work – to bring others in, rather than for me to go out.

Discipline

One of the most prominent features of monastics is the concept of discipline. This is, more than devotion, what sets monastics apart from both general practitioners and even many priests. Devotion, in the monastic, is channeled through a disciplined routine that generates a consistent rhythm of life. That rhythm of life rarely changes and dominates the monastic's everyday existence. It is within that rhythm, that discipline, that monastics describe their liberation.

What does this rhythm look like? In Pagan and polytheist monasticism, because we do not have many collective traditions (and we have a high rate of diversity under this umbrella), it looks different for each self-identified monastic person. For me, when I am practicing the way I feel best serves and pleases the Spirits I Serve, my practice includes morning and nighttime rituals, weekly periods of study and expression, and ways in which my values and sense of calling is placed in service in the ordinary world. At the heart of my discipline is a willingness to offer my whole life in service to the Spirits who claimed me. This may sound extreme; perhaps it is. I certainly cannot say it is right for others. But I know without a doubt that it was right for me. My life is Theirs, and so They are always welcome to be present with me in any moment They choose.

Because of this, my religious practice looks different from some Pagans and polytheists. While I sometimes invoke gods or other spirits, I never invoke the Spirits I Serve. They are always with me; it was part of the agreement we have. And while I invoke other spirits, such as some of the Celtic gods, I never really bid them adieu. They are thanked, but they are always welcome to stay. My home is Their home.

In the morning, I open the shrine cabinet. Water that had been blessed is poured out either outside or down the drain, with a blessing for the spirits of place and the spirits of my home. New water is poured, and the grail is placed in the shrine as I commit myself again to serving the earth. Incense and the candles, one for each of the gods, for the Spirits I Serve, for the ancestors, and for the nature spirits, are lit. I enter movement meditation, my body enacting my commitments to the elemental forces, aligning and balancing them within me. The meditation, inspired from several sources and refined over the course of years, awakens my body as a bridge between the forces of the Otherworld and ordinary life. When finished, I sit before the gods and the Spirits I Serve. I bless my ancestors, my family, my friends, my fellow Druids. The blessings are rhythmic and repetitive, allowing me to slip into a state of focusing more on the energy work around the blessings and to observe the intuitive insights into what my loved ones need, rather than the words themselves. When the time is right, I offer my prayers to the gods and Spirits I Serve – sometimes simple, sometimes complex – as I extinguish the candles, one by one:

I come before you in love and service, and ask...

Brighid, help me to feel the flame of your inspiration and the nourishing water of your healing

Lugh, help me to build my skills and serve my community well

Morrigan, Great Queen, give me courage to act and the discernment to know what right action is in these dark times

Rhiannon, bless the horses in my care and help me to cultivate their grace and nobility in myself

Cernunnos, help me to know my wild soul and to feel deep love for the wild things of the earth

> *Elen of the Ways, help me to safely tread the wild paths to the*
>   *Otherworld and back again*
> *Fair Folk, Spirits I Serve, may you live in me and through me;*
> *May my life honor Yours*
> *May I work with You to help heal the wounds in humanity*
> *The wounds that we have caused and the wounds that we carry*
> *May in healing these wounds, I approach my own divine nature*
> *And may humanity as a whole come closer to its full potential*
> *To be in service to all existences, in harmony with the earth, free*
>   *from suffering*

My hands pause on the smooth, cold glass of my ancestor and nature spirit shrine cabinet, lingering on this final meditation. I hold one last silent moment where the Spirits I Serve meet me before I leap into the busy-ness of my day.

. My morning meditation and prayer ritual recommits me to Them, and to my spiritual work in the world, every day. It reminds me that at the heart of my soul's desire is to offer my life to Them – my time, focus, and action. Daily ritual practice grounds my mundane life in mystical meaning and deeper work. While the purpose is not to cultivate better functioning in my ordinary tasks, it also affords me this additional benefit. The attentiveness, openness to inspiration and intuition, and mindfulness that I developed over the last twenty years of my evolving practice helps me to be a better teacher and researcher – but that utility is not the point of the practice. The discipline is an offering to the Spirits I love.

In acting in a disciplined way, arising from devotion to the spirits they serve, monastics provide consistent doorways throughout every day through which the Divine can enter. In that constant offering of the most precious things that humans have – our time, bodies, and attention – there is the essence of the true sacrifice, the sublimation of the small-self to the higher-self, the divine-self, the soul's work. This routine is usually combined with certain vows, which usually serve to generate a simple, conflict-free life. While the Rule by which I live is not one that is held by a collective religious group and while it does not look like a Catholic's or Buddhist's, it demands my life is given as the offering. There is an Irish triad, or wisdom saying, that has long been a source of inspiration for me in my religious life:

The three foundations of spirituality:
Hearth as altar;
Work as worship;
And service as sacrament.

My gods, the spirits of place, and the Spirits I Serve share my home (or more appropriately, They share Their home with me). My work and service in the world is infused with Their perspective, values, and guidance; in this way, I have woven together my religious and mundane lives into one relatively seamless whole.

In my own experience, discipline is by far the most difficult ideal to uphold. Life likes to intrude, and our minds like to resist our spiritual work by inserting what feels like pressing worldly concerns. For a householder (married, with a job and responsibilities) like me, it is infinitely challenging to maintain discipline. It is also deeply rewarding. It is worth noting, however, that my religious practice does not feel like a choice I made in order to feel more fulfilled. I feel that I was pursued by the Spirits I Serve from the time I was a young child. I am Theirs, and the discipline of wrapping my life around my soul's work with Them feels more like a sacred duty that my soul became indelibly wedded to many lifetimes ago. So, despite regularly failing at the fullness of what I feel that sacred duty ought to be, again and again I am called to return to my shrine room. Not only does some success yield greater results than no success, so it is worth the effort – by living life in this way, I am called to extend myself compassion, over and over, for falling short of meeting the Spirits I Serve in Their full vision for my life. Learning to be compassionate with oneself, to accept failure with equanimity and resilience, to maintain effort even when one does not feel like practicing – this builds a deep wellspring from which monastics ripple into the world.

Contemplation

At the heart of monastic discipline are periods of silence and contemplation. The core of monastic life is in listening to the divine, not reaching outward toward it. We seek to open for the divine touch, regardless of our mood, our circumstances, or our sense of inspiration. It is practicing hospitality to the spirit that called us. Maintaining long stretches of silence heightens one's sensitivity to divine wisdom. Offering periods of contemplative prayer or sitting meditation is an invitation to the divine, both immanent and transcendent, to be with us. In my experience, there is no greater gift we can give to any spirit-being than the offering of our silence and time. Other offerings are relatively easy and cheap: it takes little to pour out some whisky or light a candle. It takes a lot of effort to consistently overcome our internal resistance and sit in silence before the spirit world.

Sometimes, this is rewarded with a feeling of union and ecstasy, or a key message of wisdom, or a feeling of deep well-being and peace. But sometimes, we sit and nothing happens. Our mind wanders, we bring it back. The moments tick by. We squirm and realign ourselves. And this is fine. It is actually that squirmy, uncomfortable silent period that is the greatest offering we can give to the spirits. Because it is the most arduous and it requires the most altruistic effort. If we open the doorway to the spirit world but then slam it when they do not come bearing gifts, we are not being truly hospitable in the first place. Contemplation, if done out of devotion for one or more spirits, is much more than seeking wisdom or self-knowledge – it is a sacrificial act. Doing it many times each day for long periods, as monastic life ideally demands, is an incredible challenge that integrates devotion and discipline into periods of being rather than doing, so that Being – the Divine Mystery – might be realized.

At the end of my day, I light the candles in the shrine cabinets. The little lights in the darkness mirror the night sky outside, always a way the Spirits I Serve have communicated Their love. The darkness and light remind me of creation and destruction, life and death. As I gaze into the flames, I am taken back to the first moments of emergence, of the Divine Mystery unfolding into the abyss – and the Spirits I Serve, raw and wild and ancient, being ever reborn. I kneel in my shrine room to offer myself in my nighttime ritual: the act of listening, the gift of silence.

The morning is an outpouring of commitment and hope. The night is opening, receptive and patient. I measure my breaths, deep and slow, in and out, until I am lightly in trance. With each in-breath, I unite elemental energies with my body. With each out-breath, I send these elemental forces to the world around me. I sink deeper and deeper until my mind is comfortably quiet, open to Them. Sometimes Their insight descends as a visceral experience, or as images, or as symbols – They are too alien and non-individuated for me to understand Their touch through language. Sometimes a god interjects. Sometimes my own subconscious offers insight. Many times, I simply wait in silence before Their profound silence. The purpose is the discipline of offering myself to Them, not exactly to receive – though this is also how we have forged a way to meet across the vast chasm that is Themselves and my humanity. The offering is, as much as I can make it so, an offering of love and not expectation. I sit before Them, receptive and silent, until I feel it is time to close the ritual and either journal the insights I received or head to bed.

Contemplation is at the heart and soul of my life's work as a mystic, as well as my disciplined rhythm as a monastic. Aside from contemplative ritual practice, this stillness is woven into the fabric of my everyday life. Driving in Los Angeles traffic to work can take hours and produce anxiety or frustration. What better opportunity to practice contemplative silence and hone my ability to be patient? When I struggle and my mind is noisy and busy, I will head out to the stables to work a horse or up into the mountains to hike a trail. I bring my mind back to the present moment by becoming very mindful of my body's movements and sensations, of the horse's movements and breathing, of the world around me as I move through nature. Some nights, I sit in the recliner chair in my shrine room with my cats, stilling my mind by appreciating their soft fur and the way their purring booms in the absence of other noise. My lifelong goal is to become fully present in every moment of my life, with deep stillness at the core of my being, able to maintain being a bridge between Themselves and me indefinitely.

The Still Center

The mystery of monasticism is both in the relationship between the monastic and the spirit world and in the relationship of the monastic to humanity as a whole. I have always been a mystic, but for a number of years after I became more public in my Druidry, I thought because of my level of devotion, I ought to be a priest. Even when I was Christian, I considered the Episcopalian priesthood. It was only recently, in the last couple of years, that I have understood that it is the monastic life that calls me, not the priestly one. This makes sense when I consider my soul's work that is tied to the Spirits I Serve, and the ways that They relate to humanity. They are not beings who wish for worship or recognition or even thanks. They are ancient, from a time before the Earth was embodied in her current form and before the sun became our crystallization of light. Their work with humans is something other than rites. Their work is in interweaving Their pulse with the rhythm of humans, until we remember that we are a union of the stars and the soil. That work is not done primarily in a workshop or a ritual. It is done in silence.

For any form of monasticism, therein lies the great mystery: it is in the disciplined not-doing that Being can emerge into humanity. The monastic holds the center of that union between human and divine, having faith that they were called to that difficult, disciplined rhythm so that it might ripple outward into the world. There is a prayer in the Order of Bards, Ovates, and Druids for peace:

> *Deep within the still center of my being, may I find peace.*
> *Silently within the quiet of the Grove, may I share peace.*
> *Gently and powerfully, within the greater circle of humankind,*
>   *may I radiate peace.*

This is the heart of the monastic work: devote oneself to a rhythm that opens one to stillness, share this silently among other practitioners, radiate this gently and powerfully in human consciousness. And have faith that it matters. Even when it feels like the world is unraveling around us, sit in silence. Even when it feels like the to-do list is a mile long, sit in silence. Even when it feels like we are entirely alone, and even the spirit world has abandoned us, sit in silence. Offer the sacrifice once more, open the doorway, and wait.

Chapter 3

An Eremitic Calling: Harvest Home Hermitage

Danica Swanson interviews Patricia Christmas

Introduction

For polytheists and animists discerning a monastic calling, the lack of established monastic traditions represents one of our most daunting challenges. Modern revived polytheism is in its infancy. We have next to no religious infrastructure suitable for monastics, let alone established monasteries with provisions for guidance of religious hermits. Few options present themselves other than to forge our own way by trial and error. Given the paucity of navigational aids, what's an aspiring modern hermit to do?

Patricia Christmas, resident votary at Harvest Home Hermitage in Texas, counts herself among a handful of modern religious who explore the meaning of eremitic monasticism within a polytheistic framework. The timing of her divine nudge to go more public with her work coincided nicely with my intention to pursue something I'd wished for since I felt the first stirrings of my own calling in 2006: in-depth narrative interviews with modern polytheist monastics.

"What we are doing matters," I wrote to Patricia as we compared notes for this interview. "It's a lot of trial-and-error for now, and it's hard not to get discouraged when it seems like such an uphill climb. But if we persist, and trust the guidance we receive, perhaps we can leave some kind of lasting legacy behind for the next generation of polytheist monastic hermits, so that they might have an easier time of it than we have."

In the following interview, Patricia offers a glimpse into the challenges and rewards of developing her monastic practice "off the map."

Danica: On your blog[1] you refer to yourself as an aspiring hermit. How and when did you receive your call to monasticism, and how did you discern your call to eremitic life specifically?

Patricia: I first received what I feel was my call to this life about eight years ago. It started as just a niggling thought at the back of my mind - a draw to a kind of life that would be more dedicated and in tune with the natural rhythms of life.

I actually rejected the idea of becoming a religious hermit the first few times it came to me. It sounded nuts. I had too much going on – family, grad school, career, etc. But gradually my other pursuits either came to their natural end or moved on to a stage where they were less of a distraction. My daughter left home for college and married, and I finished my degree. And still, that niggling idea sat in the back of my mind. I finally decided that I couldn't ignore it any longer. I had worked with Habondia and Cernunnos off and on for some time, as well as another who will remain nameless. They accepted my vows on Samhain 2015.

Since then, it seems like whenever I have a need for guidance or to know which road to take next, things open up for me, though not always in expected ways. When I first decided to accept this way of life, I sat down and came up with what I would need to maintain my independence. I decided that I needed a small plot of land of between 0.75-1 acre with a very small house, located near but not within a larger city, with few or no restrictions so I could keep chickens, bees, etc., and create a garden throughout the entire property. Soon after I began looking in the Austin area for such a property, I discovered that my mother needed someone to come and live with her, to see to her daily needs, and that neither of my remaining siblings were willing to do so. I was frustrated – even furious – but it was equally important to me that Mama's wish to remain in the home my father and grandfather had built for her be respected, and that was not going to happen if I didn't make it happen. So, I bit my tongue, quit my job, and moved home with Mom. It was several months before I realized where I was: in a small house on 0.8 acre of land, near but not in a large city, with few restrictions on land use. I hadn't specified that it shouldn't be my childhood home.

Danica: Do you present yourself as an aspiring monastic when you're outside your Hermitage? If so, how has that been received?

Patricia: Not generally. My concept of a hermit is as an invisible religious. My Work and relationships with my Goddesses and Gods are very personal and don't require outside acknowledgment. Others' Work might require a certain amount of public attention in order to be accomplished, but mine doesn't, and that's how I'm most comfortable.

Danica: Do you wear special clothing associated with monastic practice such as head coverings, veils, prayer shawls, tunics, or nun habits?

Patricia: No, I don't have anything like this. Generally speaking, the types of garb used by monastics tend to be simplified and practical versions of whatever people were wearing in the place and time in which they started. My own clothing is similar.

Danica: You wrote in one of your blog entries: "It might seem odd that an unapologetically Pagan (aspiring) hermit should turn to the wisdom of other faiths, but there are precious few Pagan monastics out there, and we're all currently in the same small boat – feeling a desperate need for our kind of spiritual expression within our faith community, but forced to set sail with very few navigational aids."

What forms of monasticism do you draw from? Do you have any role models?

Patricia: I draw quite a lot from the Western traditions of monasticism, which is not surprising since this is my primary culture. Cosmology and traditions may differ, but the actual experience of eremitic life – the struggles with cultural norms and with acedia for instance – are very similar. Right now, I'm reading a memoir by Sr. Elizabeth Wagner called *Seasons in my Garden: Meditations from a Hermitage*.[2] Some sections are not relevant to me at all, but many have been of great assistance. I'm particularly drawn to a quote she includes from another religious thinker, Adrian Van Kamm: "Our limits are the outline of our vocation." I've spent this past year struggling with limits – both setting them and running up against them. I found her discussion of this subject very meaningful.

Danica: What's a typical day like for you at Harvest Home Hermitage?

Patricia: I have several different typical days, depending on what is needed, and I fear they may all disappoint those looking for something overwhelmingly "holy." Generally speaking, prayers and meditation times tend to happen on the spur of the moment rather than by schedule.

On days when I'm working from my home office, I tend to rise by 7:30 am. I have a short morning prayer period until 8 am. I spend an hour either working in the garden or studying, depending on the weather, then move into the office and get to work. I spend the hours between 9 am and 5 pm working, with breaks for lunch with my sister and afternoon yoga. After that, it's dinner and then Wheel of Fortune as an amusement. I may also do light housework or knit or watch a movie after dinner, although as the days are getting shorter, I find myself retiring to bed not long after sundown, so am often in bed by 8 pm or so.

Field days are less focused, but also give me far more solitude. I'm generally up and out the door by 8 am. I work on my various projects throughout the day, often ending with the setting of the sun, since it's hard to dig shovel tests after dark. Generally, I'm in quite out of the way areas and entirely on my own, so I tend to get a lot of quiet thought time on these days. Field days may last one day or extend over several depending on the amount of work and distance traveled. Just because I'm out of the Hermitage, however, doesn't mean that I lose sight of the Work. It's the work I do as an archaeologist that enables me to do the Work I need to do at the Hermitage.

As for most folks, weekends tend to be errand days – grocery shopping is a favorite outing for my sister, and very important to her, since she can no longer drive. This tends to be a time when we spend longer times talking, watching movies, or playing board games.

Danica: Is your practice guided by a monastic rule? If so, how did you determine that rule, and how does it shape your practice?

Patricia: Monastic rules are structures that come about in response to the stresses and needs of a specific community or individual. Probably the classic Western example of a monastic rule is that of the Benedictines. What many don't realize is that St. Benedict only formalized a monastic rule toward the end of his life, and it was based on what had worked for the community he led.

My practice is still evolving, so the short answer is no, I don't have a specific rule that I follow. Even well-thought-out plans have a way of falling apart when faced with the reality of daily living. I do have a daily schedule that has arisen from an attempt to force some semblance of work-life balance. Working from home really means living at the office and the temptation is to be always on the job. Setting a series of alarms to nudge me to do things like eat, exercise, spend some time in the garden, or read and relax, have turned out to be necessary. Otherwise, I tend to work myself into the ground and a lot of things get neglected.

Danica: Models of monastic life in other religions - especially for hermits - typically involve vows of celibacy and renunciation of family or "householder" life. Does this apply to your practice? Why or why not?

Patricia: Not a renunciation, per se, but definitely a sort of withdrawal. When I first began to feel the stirrings of my call, one of the excuses I used for not answering it was that my daughter and son-in-law lived close by, and I had a new grandson to help raise. Within a month of my coming up with that excuse, my son-in-law received a job offer that was simply too good to be ignored – in Hong Kong! So much for that excuse!

On the other hand, I've never spent so much time with my immediate family as I have after making my vows. I suddenly found myself thrust into the role of the family caregiver. First my mother, who was diagnosed with congestive heart failure, began showing signs of decline to the point that she needed someone to live with her. After Mama passed on, my eldest sister (in her 70s) began to show signs of early dementia as well as having a heart condition of her own and is now in my care. This is a situation I never expected to find myself in, but I am taking it as part of my Work as a solitary religious, as well as an education on things to come in my own life. It's saved me from my own worst excesses as I move into this life and, of course, it's also forcing me to work through family issues that I have been avoiding.

As for vows of celibacy, I don't see much point to them within the context of my Wiccan religious paradigm. That kind of restriction is very much a product of the transcendent religions, where the physical and spiritual worlds are separate and often set in opposition. Now, I do feel a need for solitude to do my Work, as it's being revealed to me, which tends to be along the lines of land and house tending, elder care, and contemplation. Celibacy is more a means to an end rather than a deliberate renunciation and, frankly, I don't feel any sense of loss associated with that.

Danica: What are the biggest challenges and deepest rewards you experience as an aspiring hermit monastic?

Patricia: The biggest challenge for me has been one of trust. Taking a religious vow means turning over the reins of life to Another – to whatever deities one swears themselves to. It means no longer being in control and trusting that wherever you end up and whatever you end up doing will be where you are needed most, and where your talents are best put to use. This may mean embracing a life you would never have considered, living in a place you had never considered. It also means that you just have to trust that, even if you can't see the big Why of what you have been asked to do or the position in which you find yourself, the Ones to which you are sworn do, and They will make it possible.

Learning to release those reins, conversely, has also been one of the greatest rewards. I'm a natural control freak and a great worrier. Learning to let it all go and just go where They lead is at once terrifying and liberating.

Danica: You wrote that Harvest Home Hermitage is "dedicated to the worship of the Goddess Habondia and the God Cernunnos. Like any hermitage, it is both a physical and a spiritual place, one that abides with the hermit regardless of whether the hermit is actually abiding in any particular physical place."

What does this dual concept of hermitage mean to you? What is it that endures about your hermitage regardless of its physical location?

Patricia: The morning after I took my vows, a sentence in a book leapt out at me: "Sacred space is within you now." I didn't read anything that came after it, because I had an immediate sense that it was unimportant. This simple sentence was the intended message: that the actual space in which a hermit abides, while meaningful and necessary, is far less important than the sacred space the hermit cultivates within themselves. Harvest Home is important. The land needs to be honored, to be given space to heal. The creatures of the land, both of this realm and the Other, need a place of sanctuary. But if I were to be forced to uproot by some circumstance outside my control, the Hermitage would also travel with me.

Danica: Could you say a bit about where Harvest Home Hermitage is located? What factors enable you to pursue a monastic way of life in this location?

Patricia: Harvest Home Hermitage is located just outside of the Houston city limits, near the San Jacinto River. This area has been heavily industrialized over the past sixty or more years, and while the pollution levels have diminished somewhat over the past couple of decades, there are many things I can remember as a girl that simply aren't here anymore: fireflies, Spanish moss, and cypress so thick that you had to search to find glimpses of the water in the river as you traveled over the IH-10 bridge. Many of the trees have been cut down or have died due to drought and sickness. This lot is one of the few that still has a thick stand of oaks and pines covering the back 1/3 of the property. There is nothing to shelter the front of the property and the sound of the highway is a constant hum. This is land that needs someone to treat it with respect and kindness, to limit the chemical assaults by as much as they can, to allow the land to begin to heal. I can't hope to have an effect on a large scale, but healing can start small. It can start with this piece of land, this one not-quite-an-acre.

Harvest Home Hermitage is also the home in which I was raised. The land was bought by my grandfather in the 1930s. The house was built in 1953 by my father and grandfather using lumber milled from trees that grew on this land. Admittedly, that's not much of a history, but it is three generations of family and counting. The occasional hammer divots were put there by my father and grandfather. The tiny inked lines in the casing of the kitchen door mark the growth of my brother and sisters, myself, my daughter, my grandson, and assorted nieces and grandnephews. The Dutch iris and guernsey lilies were planted by my grandparents, the paperwhites and ferns by my mother, the roses by me.

From a practical standpoint, Harvest Home Hermitage is also a good fit. The land is big enough to have gardens to help produce some food and herbs, to have fruit trees and eventually a labyrinth walk, but not so large that I won't be able to take care of it into the future. It's in the county in an area without homeowner associations, and so is not subject to much regulation about what can be done on the property. It's close enough to a large city that not only can I find work to support myself and the Hermitage, but I also have access to medical care and other amenities that will make life healthy and interesting for the sister I care for, and for me when I finally need them. And frankly, it's a far better house and land than I could afford to buy on my own.

Harvest Home is a place where I feel close to my ancestors, that has what I need to be comfortable, and – most of all – that needs me and the Work I'm doing. Finally, there is one last feature that makes Harvest Home Hermitage the best place for me – it's where the Goddess and the God put me.

Danica: How strict are you about maintaining an eremitic life? Do you have any hopes or plans to join forces with other polytheists/hermits/monastics?

Patricia: An eremitic life is my ultimate goal. Right now, due to family and career constraints, it sometimes feels like a very distant goal. I'm not averse to the occasional visitor but have no interest in building a physical community around Harvest Home, although I certainly see some of the benefits of laura-type situations.[3]

Danica: What suggestions do you have for polytheists called to monastic life in general, and eremitic life specifically?

Patricia:
1. Don't expect this life to go according to your plan. It won't. I can pretty much guarantee that however you envision your life as a Pagan or polytheist monk, nun, hermit, avowed religious, or whatever you want to call it, it will not turn out as you plan. It will turn out as They plan. Get used to that idea early.

2. Don't go into this kind of life expecting to become someone you aren't. You will not float through life on clouds of enlightenment. If anything, you will become much more who you already are because you'll be stripping away the distractions and facades. If you don't like that person, then you have more personal work to do and should examine your motivations closely. Monastic or eremitic life will not "fix" you. It will not make you more

spiritual. It will not make you a better, more balanced person.

Do expect to find and identify every single one of your faults and shortcomings. Eremitic life is a great way to find the limits of your ability. This is important, because knowing what you can't do is at least as important as knowing what you can. You will also find out what you can do, because They aren't going to entrust Work to someone who can't manage it. After three years, I am in essence the same generally pragmatic, irritable, occasionally impatient and often sarcastic old crone I was before I took vows. I'm just that person with Purpose.

Danica: Is there anything you'd like to comment on that I didn't ask about? If so, please add it in!

Patricia: Some months ago, I was feeling a bit low and adrift, and entered a meditation with the question on my mind of "Why? Why am I doing this? What's the point?" The answer I received is one I feel drawn to share. Bits of it are embarrassingly frou-frou but bear with me.

In this meditation, I became a fish, a salmon. I swam up a river that became increasingly rough. There were steep drops and rapids, all of which I swam and leaped through to reach a spring high in the mountains. There was a small pool that had formed around the mouth of the spring, and it was lined with Herkimer diamonds, double-pointed crystals that glittered in the sun. Once there, I crawled out of the pool onto land and became a beaver. As a beaver, I felled a few of the small trees around the pool and built a nest. The water backed up and created a still pond that rose a bit then cascaded over the dam and returned to its course. Further downstream were other beavers, also going about their business of building nests and incidentally creating these still pools. This continued down the length of the river – a cascade of water slowed by gentle pools, one after the other. As I watched, animals emerged to drink from the pools.

I was told to notice that while the water was rushing past, only a few could drink. Those who were too small or not well-suited could be tossed about or drowned, dashed against the rocks by the uncontrolled current. Where the water was slow, pooled behind the beaver dams, any could come and take what they needed. The real point is that none of these animals had any real idea of why the water had slowed. They couldn't see the beaver down in her nest. They only saw that the water that had once been too swift to drink safely was now within reach.

This may not be the most original of imagery and my 1980s New Agey background is definitely on display, but the message I took from it is something I feel is important for those of us pioneering this path. The message for those of us on this polytheistic/Pagan monastic journey is this: It doesn't matter if no one else ever knows who or what you are, or what you're doing. It doesn't matter if you retreat to the wilds or into an urban apartment and never speak to another human soul again, if that is your Work. Even unseen, what you are doing has an impact. It affects the world around you. It helps to shape reality in ways we may not be able to understand at the current moment, in ways that will make access to the Ones we serve easier and more nurturing for those around us. It is important.

Stay in your Cell (whatever that may be). Do your Work. Trust.

Endnotes

1   https://harvesthomehermitage.wordpress.com/blog/
2   *Seasons in my Garden: Meditations from a Hermitage*. Elizabeth Wagner. Ave Maria Press. 2016.
3   A "laura" is a monastic community in which the members each live in their own cell or cave, but come together for worship. (ed)

Chapter 4

Modern Polytheistic Monasticism: A Revolutionary Vision

Syren Nagakyrie

There are growing numbers of people interested in a polytheistic monastic lifestyle, or at least growing awareness of it as a possibility. Many of these modern would-be monastics lead a life in which devotion is present in every daily activity, service to others is considered service to the divine, and hours are spent in study, devotion, and contemplation rather than excessive socializing or other external activities.

While the modern polytheist monastic movement is very young, we may reflect on thousands of years of monastic tradition; we are not confined to examples of Christian monasticism. Monastic lineages have existed in India, Japan, and other cultures since long before the advent of Christianity. The central principles of these traditions – discernment, detachment, spiritual virtue and well-being, and devotion to service and divinity – provide an excellent basis for the development of polytheist monasticism. They represent core values that move us away from immersion in the materialistic world and towards spiritual development.

People choose to enter monastic life for a number of reasons, but certainly withdrawal from worldly expectations is a common one. Many monastically-inclined people find the pressure to participate in social life, generate monetary wealth, and constantly be productive to be too much of a distraction from their spiritual life. They feel unfulfilled in the lifestyle that is elevated by American culture and are looking for a framework that resists these expectations and allows them to commit to spiritual practice. The monastic lifestyle is a powerful resistance; indeed, it goes against almost everything mainstream culture values. For this reason, monasticism can also be a haven for the marginalized and disenfranchised.

I see four main areas of resistance in which a monastic lifestyle serves:

Resistance to the exploitation of time and labor

Our time is one of the most precious gifts that we have. Why should we spend it in service to lining the pockets of the wealthy, when we could spend it in service to the divine and each other? Our time is not a commodity to be traded and our productivity does not determine our worth as human beings. Our existence, our innate divinity and connection with the divine, is sacrosanct. The monastic is not interested in accumulating unnecessary wealth, in owning more than is needed for basic needs, or in engaging in activities that do not support devotion and service. The monastic's productive time and labor is committed to meeting their own and other's basic needs to allow space to open for contemplation and devotion – no more and no less.

This commitment requires vigilance. In a capitalist culture, the monastic must practice intentionality in their daily life to make sure they do not fall into the trap of consumerism. This is not to say the monastic does not consume, or that their labor never goes towards resource-generating pursuits. Monastics must support themselves, particularly when living in solitude or practicing their lifestyle outside of a community (which is the majority of animist and polytheist monastics). But the focus of consumption for a monastic must remain on meeting daily needs and resource-generation must be for the benefit of those who lack access. In this way, a monastic lifestyle can also uplift marginalized people.

Resistance to the disenchantment of daily life

Our modern lifestyles leave little time for appreciation and connection with each other, the world around us, and the divine. Our power as creative beings in relation with a great web of existence is reduced to a few shallow moments that we can wring from the constant pressure to produce and do and go-go-go. This disenchantment, this disconnection from who we are, is the core of the systems that harm us. The monastic who steps back from the external pressure, finds joy in the simplicity of daily life, and re-enchants their days with deep contemplation and connection with beings human and more-than-human holds a key to remembering our true selves. Like The Hermit card, they hang a lamp showing us the way.

Monastics bring enchantment back to the community. As devotionalists and frequent mystics, they serve as a bridge between the mundane and the sacred, bringing the sacred into the everyday and making every day sacred. Through their creativity and service, they make a connection with the divine more readily available, and in contemplation they access deep truths and awareness.

As capitalism continues to exploit people of their labor, the desire for re-enchantment of daily life will certainly increase. The resources developed through practice by monastic communities – solitude, devotion, simplicity – are difficult, but not impossible, to commodify. Monastic communities must take care to not fall into the trap of commodifying their resources for profit.

Resistance to oppression and the devaluation of all beings

As Silence Maestas wrote:

"Devotion is not easily approached when one is hungry, fearful, injured, in pain, grieving, angry, or depressed. One cannot focus on cultivating sacred relationship or even on simply associating with sacred spaces when you are worried for your life, the lives of your family members, and the lives of people who look like you."[1]

I have experienced this myself. While in, and recovering from, my abusive marriage, and while faced with the financial and housing instability that resulted from my divorce, surrender has been incredibly difficult. If we want more people to be able to lead spiritual lives, we have to make sure their basic needs and safety are assured. By being a model of true simple living and resource-sharing, monastics help shift the narrative of who is deserving and valuable in society.

If one truly believes that all humans contain some spark or connection with the divine, then anything that harms and oppresses humanity should be revolutionized. Those of us who place ourselves in service to the divine are also placing ourselves in service to humanity. Not only out of compassion for other humans, but out of love for deity. This orientation towards service can help reduce the structural barriers that contribute to oppression. But monastics must be careful not to take too much of a "charity" or "missionary" approach. This approach may help with a few immediate needs - providing a bowl of food to a hungry person, for example - but it often comes at a cost to the people being served. We have countless examples of religious communities who receive great financial support and engage in activities that do nothing to improve the overall conditions of peoples' lives. Polytheistic monastics have an opportunity to do better.

Resistance to resource extraction from the earth

Many pagan monastics regard all parts of nature, moving and unmoving, as having their own unique spirit; all beings on this planet are sacred. So, the monastic also aligns themselves with the earth and the beings of the place in which they live. The pagan monastic is often inclined to spend time in contemplative appreciation of the wild and natural world which we are a part of, and to protect and learn from those places.

Joan Chittister writes in *In the Heart of the Temple: my spiritual vision for today's world*[2]

"In an age that preaches the gospel of rugged individualism and 'free-market' capitalism, monastic spirituality is a gift thrown again at the feet of a society made poor for the sake of the oligarchy of the wealthy. [It] stands with simplicity in the face of greed, conspicuous consumption, and the gorging off two-thirds of the resources of the world by one-third of the people of the world, Europeans and North Americans. The simple fact is that none of us can in conscience consume what belongs by human right to another."

The concept of extraction and exploitation is in stark contrast to the values of service and devotion. Thus, the monastic practices an anti-capitalist resistance, though often without naming it that way. As such, this lifestyle is not easily accomplished in this society. There are many systemic barriers, external and internal. But the call to create a contemplative life firmly rooted in devotion and service is strong. By developing a strong relationship with place and allying ourselves against the decimation of the planet, animist and polytheist monastics place themselves in service to the spirits of the land. This relationship can help deepen the monastics' spiritual life while ensuring future monastics have a place to pursue their own paths.

My Path to Monasticism

My commitment to developing a monastic lifestyle was invigorated following a period of trauma and insecurity, including a sudden death in my immediate family, divorce from an abusive spouse, and housing insecurity. This time has been clarifying and informative alongside terrifying; the ongoing process of shedding my old life, my old expectations, my old attachments has been difficult and painful. I have spent the last two years in relative solitude and have experienced joy, contentment, and loneliness. The loneliness, however is not new – being dependent upon an abusive husband and abusive wage labor jobs for security, caring about other peoples' perceptions of me and my work, forcing myself to be productive when my spirit was screaming for time to just be, was even more lonely and isolating. Upon realizing this, and the harm I was causing myself, I embraced my situation as an opportunity for healing and transformation. Yet, it must be acknowledged that embracing the situation would have been impossibly difficult if it were not for the generosity of friends and strangers who provided support in many ways. It is only through supporting one another that we can overcome the structural barriers to devotion.

As I allow this process to unfold, the call to live my most authentic life becomes stronger. A contemplative life of devotion and service is a life that feels right and good to me, a life that engages in as little harm as possible and is aligned with my values and connection with the earth. One of the things that I gained in coming out of an abusive relationship was an unwillingness to harbor abuse towards myself or abuse towards others. I cannot harbor blame against myself and I cannot willingly subject myself to something that I know will bring deep pain for minimal reward.

This too is not easy in our culture. The culture of the United States, so deeply rooted in capitalism and colonialism, is incredibly coercive and abusive. Wage labor is one of the most coercive aspects of capitalism: requiring us to be in service to capital or risk starvation. What do we lose, what potential does not get realized, while all of us are working ourselves to exhaustion in service to capital? That is not the practice of service I am here for. I am not here to bow to kings and capitalists. The cost to all of us is too great.

And yet, we still live in a capitalist society. There is no opting out, there is no freedom to choose; there is no true consent. So, what does this mean for someone who wants to live a monastic lifestyle? How can I best move into this space of deepening into my truth and purpose and doing my true Work, while also meeting my basic needs within a society that puts a price tag on existence?

I'm most interested in creating a life in which wage labor is minimally necessary, if at all. The past two years have certainly shown me that I can make do with far less than I thought I needed, that indeed I can be very happy by fulfilling my basic needs.

So, what does the material foundation of a monastic life look like to me? It is pretty simple really:

- Land that is my own/held in common/conservation with other people.
- A small house or other structure.
- Labor focused on meeting needs, trade and self-employment service-oriented income to meet remaining needs, occasional supplementation with wage labor.

I envision communities that are supportive of solitude and spiritual service, with access to a beautiful expanse of land, to be in a relationship of reciprocity with people and place. I hope to see this community manifest, for myself and others, in my lifetime.

In the interim, I am working on creating as much of this contemplative life of devotion and service as I can. I'm removing my own blocks and barriers to practice, feeling into where my service is most needed now, and opening to divine and ancestral guidance. I can only continue to flow where the current takes me, remaining hopeful that when it comes time to leap, my Divine Mother will open Her hands. I will continue to resist the conscription of my time, the chaining of my spirit to capitalism as much as I can.

Endnotes

1   https://walkingtheheartroad.com/2016/08/14/devotional-justice/
2   *In the Heart of the Temple: my spiritual vision for today's world.* Joan Chittister. Bluebridge. 2004

Chapter 5

Building a Druid Monastic Practice

Julie Bond

I became a novice in the Order of the Sacred Nemeton (OSN), a contemplative Druid monastic Order, in 2010 and took my full vows in 2012, but I had been working on my own to develop a Druid monastic practice for many years prior to that. I began studying monastic practice (mostly Christian) in the 1990's, during which time I also began the Ovate Grade of the Order of Bards, Ovates, and Druids (OBOD).

At the time, I felt like a minority of one as far as interest in Druidic monasticism was concerned, but the process of developing my practice was very satisfying. I had long felt a pull towards a life of deep spiritual meaning and order. Monasticism seemed to satisfy these yearnings. It felt like my vocation, and has continued to do so.

Throughout the process of building a Druid monastic practice it felt very important to be faithful to what I was learning as a Druid, not simply adopt practices from other traditions and religions. Anything I found in other traditions had to be able to fit within Druidry.

Developing the Basic Practices

I started by studying various Christian monastic Orders (primarily the Benedictines, Cistercians, and Carthusians), looking at their daily timetables and forms of prayer. I saw that often their prayer times were linked to daily cycles like Dawn, Dusk, Midday, and Midnight – which were highly relevant to Druid practice.

This Dawn, Dusk, Midday and Midnight structure became the framework I decided to build on. But what should I do at those times? The schedule fit within Druid practice, but the prayers and readings didn't have an equivalent. I didn't have a set of "Druid psalms" to use, and the Triads didn't seem like a suitable substitute. I had a framework but wondered what to put on it.

The answer came from my Ovate study. One of the practical exercises was called "In the Eye of the Sun." It suggested sitting facing the relevant direction for the time of day (Midnight-North, Dawn-East, Midday-South, Dusk-West) and simply keeping your attention focused on something like your breath. If your attention wandered, you should just notice the fact and then bring it back to the focus. I don't think the expectation was that people should do four meditations a day, but for me four daily meditation times was a perfect structure to develop my Druid monastic practice on. So, perhaps appropriately, my monastic practice grew from silence. I was on my way!

Over time these daily meditations, which I called Observances, developed to include spoken prayers and invocations.

I began by adding a list of Correspondences to the beginning of each session. These were based on the associations for the Elements, Earth, Water, Air and Fire listed in the first version of the OBOD Bardic Grade Workbook. For example, the list for the Midnight Observance was:

- North
- Alban Arthan
- Death and Rebirth
- Opening to the forces of Inspiration and Conception
- Mistletoe
- Conception/Incarnation
- The Light of Arthur
- "In the stillness of Night is intuition born"
- Earth – feminine, receptive, grounded, the physical body
- The Mineral kingdom
- Crown chakra

For each Observance I would light a candle on my main shrine, face the relevant direction, read the Correspondences list thoughtfully, and then sit for a period of silent meditation.

I liked that the day could be seen as a "year in miniature," with the four daily Observances corresponding to the significant markers of the year: Midnight-Winter Solstice, Dawn-Spring Equinox, Midday-Summer Solstice, Dusk-Autumn Equinox. This brought to mind the cross-quarter festivals: Imbolc, Beltane, Lughnasadh, and Samhuinn. I decided that Observances corresponding to these festivals could be fitted in between the four main Observances each day. In order to keep things manageable, I decided to keep these extra Observances to set times. The Early Morning Observance I added to the end of the Midnight Observance, mainly to allow for a sensible amount of sleep. The Late Morning Observance I set for 9am, the Afternoon Observance at 3pm, and the Late Evening Observance at 9pm. These additional Observances might correspond with what some Christian monastics call their "little Offices."

I didn't do the silent meditation period for the 'little' Observances. Instead, I did a meditation/prayer with prayer-beads for the Early Morning Observance, and had study periods during the Late Morning and Afternoon Observances. The Late Evening Observance was mainly an acknowledgement of the stopping of activity and preparation for sleep. I also put together lists of correspondences for these additional Observances. I didn't have material from the OBOD workbook to use, but I wrote the lists using the same themes, with the addition of the relevant moon phase. For example, the list for the Late Morning Observance was:

- Southeast
- Beltane
- Burgeoning growth and greenery
- The Green Man

- The Lovers: Union of Polarities
- Opening to Sensuality
- Vibrant green
- Early youth: 14-21 years
- Sacral/Belly chakra
- The Full Moon
- Fire

I now had an eight-fold daily Observance. At this stage I tended to stick to set times for the Observances: Midnight Observance at Midnight, Early Morning Observance immediately after the Midnight Observance (1am), Dawn Observance at 6am, Late Morning Observance at 9am, Midday Observance at Midday, Afternoon Observance at 3pm, Dusk Observance at 6pm, and Late Evening Observance at 9pm.

As I continued working with the daily Observances I added to the spoken words, usually drawing inspiration from the OBOD ceremonies I was working with. For example, at the beginning of the Midnight Observance I began to use the opening:

"Facing the place of the starry night sky, of midnight, of Alban Arthan, of winter, I greet the spirits of the North and of the Element Earth. Dear Spirits, I send you my love and greetings and ask that my Intuition might shine within my Spirit."

I followed this with a short visualization connecting with the Element Earth, visualizing the Pole-Star rising high above in the night sky, and feeling strongly connected to my intuition. I used similar openings for the other main Observances, but didn't add them to the 'little' Observances.

One of the important features of almost every OBOD ceremony was "Giving Peace to the Quarters," and it wasn't long before I added this to the four main Observances. I gave Peace to each of the quarters, followed by "May there be peace throughout the whole world" facing the direction of that Observance. For the little Observances I simply said "May there be Peace throughout the whole world" facing the relevant direction.

After this I added a slightly altered version of the Druid Prayer at the beginning of each Observance.

Grant, if it be thy will, O Great Shining Ones, thy Protection;
And in Protection, Strength;
And in Strength, Humility;
And in Humility, Understanding;
And in Understanding, Knowledge;
And in Knowledge, the Knowledge of Right Action;
And in the Knowledge of Right Action, the Love of it;
And in the Love of it, the Love of all Existences;
And in the Love of all Existences, the Love of the Gods and
   of all Goodness.
So May it Be.

The next development was adding prayers for others. For the four main Observances I focused on praying for the Elemental kingdoms. For the little Observances I focused my prayers on the yearly cycle and life stages.

- Midnight Observance: for the mineral kingdom
- Early Morning Observance: for all young creatures
- Dawn Observance: for the human kingdom
- Late Morning Observance: for all lovers
- Midday Observance: for the animal kingdom
- Afternoon Observance: for harvest and families
- Dusk Observance: for the plant kingdom
- Late-Evening Observance: for all those approaching and crossing the threshold from one life to the next

Again, these attributions came from my Druid studies. My

daily timetable developed to include more formal work periods which could include all sorts of activities, including household tasks. Study periods tended to concentrate on my OBOD course work in the early years and later my OSN work. The times of the Observances kept it all on track and were constant reference points to return to throughout the day.

Cycles of Time

As my monastic practice deepened, I began to feel that I should be doing the Dawn Observances actually at dawn and the Dusk Observances at dusk. This would mean a shifting timetable as I live in the UK and there is quite a large variation in the times of dawn and dusk throughout the year. This developed into alternating periods of "Solstitial Stability" and "Equinoctial Change." The daily timetable was fixed around the times of the Solstices, but around the Equinoxes the times of the Dawn and Dusk Observances changed week by week. I limited the time changes to half hours so it didn't get horrendously complicated.

The annual clock change between Greenwich Mean Time and British Summer Time added an additional complication. To continue to do the Midday Observance at 12pm once we moved into British Summer Time would not have reflected actual midday, so I moved it to 1pm and the Midnight Observance to 1am. I then had a Winter Daily Round and a Summer Daily Round.

Winter Daily Round
12am-1am: Midnight Observance
1am-1:30am: Early Morning Observance
1:30am-6am: Sleep
(Dawn Observance moved through the Winter between 6.30am and 9am and was fitted in at the correct time.)
Following Dawn Observance: Breakfast
8am-9am: Cleaning/Work

9am-10am: Late Morning Observance followed by study/ reading

10am-12pm: Work/Cleaning

12pm-12:30pm: Midday Observance

12:30pm-1pm: Midday Meal

1pm-3pm: Work

3pm-4pm: Afternoon Observance followed by study/reading (Dusk Observance moved through the Winter between 3.30pm and 6pm and was fitted in at the correct time.)

4pm-5pm: Work

7pm-9pm: Recreation/Reading/Craftwork/Music practice

9pm-9:30pm: Late Evening Observance

9:30pm: Personal Night Prayers

10pm-12am: Sleep

The Summer Daily Round was very similar, but I added a rest break in the middle of the day to compensate for the earlier times of rising for the Dawn Observance.

Further Developments

My basic practices were set, but I continued to add new elements to the Observances over time. A Daily Dedication and a prayer giving thanks and asking for blessings on the coming day were added to the Midnight Observance, as I saw that as the beginning of the daily round. I added Greetings to the Moon to the little Observances. I decided to say a prayer called The Illumination of Lights during the Early Morning Observance instead of the Druid Prayer, which I had just said at the beginning of the Midnight Observance. I added the Desiderata to the end of the Dawn Observance, as I felt it set a good tone for facing the day and its coming challenges. The Blessing of Beginnings became part of the Early Morning Observance. In the Late Evening Observance, I added a prayer of thanksgiving, intercessions for the various Elemental kingdoms, a daily review, a wishing of peace to the Ancestors, the Druid Peace Prayer, and a prayer as preparation for sleep.

I also started to perform a more formal beginning to each Observance by grounding and centering, and a more formal ending by blowing out the shrine candle and repeating "May the world be filled with peace and love and light" three times. These too were taken from my OBOD work.

Silence and Seasonal Festivals

In addition to the daily round, I wanted to add regular retreat periods to my monastic practice. The most obvious periodic marker throughout the year seemed to be the Dark (New) Moon, so I began to observe silent days during that time.

The practice of keeping silence began to play a larger part in my monastic work over the years, and I started observing the Great Silence from the end of each Late Evening Observance until the end of the Dawn Observance (except for speech during the Observances themselves). In addition to not speaking, this meant no longer using audio books to help me go to sleep or listening to manufactured sound such as CDs or the radio.

As the year turned, I was, of course, celebrating the seasonal festivals, using slightly adapted forms of the OBOD solo ceremonies. I tried to keep these days as clear of other commitments as possible. In line with my practice of linking each festival to a specific time of day, I started performing the festival ceremonies at those particular times. This added an extra depth to the ceremonies, although Imbolc and the Spring Equinox could be a bit of a challenge! For each of the Solstices I began to do an all-night vigil, an idea which came from the OBOD ceremonial work which suggests an all-night vigil for the Summer Solstice. I had been doing that for some years before I added an all-night vigil for the Winter Solstice. This is very long here in the UK – from just before 4pm until around 8am the next morning - but performing the Winter Solstice ceremony at Midnight helps to break it up a little. During the all-night vigils I tend to relax the Great Silence and listen to recordings of traditional stories such as the Mabinogion.

The Breviary

I put together a small folder or 'breviary' containing my daily Observances, which was useful not only at home but when I went out during the day. I could quietly pray the Observances anywhere: on trains or buses, in parks, or even in busy city squares. Taking my prayers out into the city felt good. I would try to find a suitable place at the relevant times to stop and unobtrusively pray the Observances. It required me to plan ahead, but I found many little green places which were very suitable. It wasn't always ideal but a certain amount of pragmatism was needed. Praying the Observances on railway station platforms, crowded trains, and buses, was not ideal but it was better than missing the regular prayer times altogether. It also felt calming in the often-chaotic atmosphere of a busy and crowded city.

For the early breviary I used small clip-files (like Filofax folders). I added a suitable picture at the beginning of each Observance, and also had pictures, often of deities, at the front of the breviary itself. I used the index tabs to create sections for the Druid prayer beads I had made, inspiring texts, and meditations for use during the seasonal ceremonies.

The Habit

In the midst of developing my daily Observances, I started wearing habit-like garments: a long shift/dress, a shorter tunic over that, a cowl and hood, and a rope belt. These were all black as that seemed to be both practical and sacred: relating to the dark and fruitful Earth and to the darkness from which all creation came. Additionally, the Roman writer Tacitus mentioned Druid women on Anglesey wearing black. In winter the tunic, cowl, and hood were wool/acrylic which I knitted myself. In the summer I wore cotton/linen. At first, I used extra-large t-shirts as tunics, but later on I bought them from a company that makes historical garments. I made the belt from cotton yarn using the French-knitting technique. For footwear I used flat, black lace-up shoes or boots, (as I continue to do now even though I now wear the habit of the Order of the Sacred Nemeton). I will buy leather ones as long as they are from second-hand or charity shops but if I buy any new, which is very rare, I avoid buying leather because it is an animal product and its production involves great cruelty. I have soft-soled sandals which I wear when moving around for the Midnight Observances as I live in a flat on the second floor of a building and don't want to disturb my neighbors at night. I call these my 'night shoes' and I change into them just before beginning of the Late Evening Observance, then back into my day shoes after breakfast.

In addition, I had and continue to use, a long, black, tabard-like garment which can be put on and taken off fairly quickly for the Midnight and Early Morning Observances: a quite heavy one for use in the winter and a lighter one for the summer. I tend to call them my 'night habit'.

In adopting the early habit, I was looking at practicality, protection, and protest (against what has come to be called "fast fashion"). Wearing a habit helps to simplify my life. I no longer have to worry about shopping for clothes, and the question "What shall I wear?" for any particular occasion is already answered. I wore my early habit all the time, including in work places, as I now continue to wear the OSN habit. People do sometimes ask about it, but if people are genuinely interested, I don't mind explaining that I am a Druid nun.

Mending the habit became an important activity in order to make the garments last, which saves money and means that clothes don't get thrown away. Any parts which become beyond repair I use in craft projects such as making rag-rugs or patchwork. Remaining scraps become stuffing for meditation cushions. Making and mending the habit has helped with my craft skills, which feels like an important aspect of both my Druid and monastic work.

Adapting into the Order of the Sacred Nemeton

After I joined the OSN, I of course had to adapt my practices to fit with the Order's. The Observances as constant reference points throughout the day continued in the OSN's four-fold Daily Offices. I have kept some of my earlier practices and added them to the OSN Offices, including my little Observances. I had also to change from my early habit to the OSN habit which is quite different (a long tunic, scapular with hood, and a cincture, all made from unbleached linen).

Making the shift wasn't as difficult as it might seem, as I was able to adapt my practices gradually throughout my novitiate. The OSN rituals and theory have a more ADF/Henge of Keltria flavor than that of OBOD, which has given me new perspectives on Druidry, and I have been able to incorporate some of my OBOD learning into my OSN practices. Blending the two systems has worked well for me, has added depth to my Druid practice, and feels more complete.

Living as a Druid monastic is the core of my life. Even during times of serious illness, when I have been unable to do my monastic practice fully, I have always maintained the intention of eventually returning to full practice. When I can't do the physical practices, I still maintain my spiritual focus. I can no longer imagine living my life in any other way: my days moving through the sequence of the Daily Offices, and the year unfolding through the sequence of the lunar months and the seasonal celebrations.

I couldn't feel 'right' living any other way.

Chapter 6

Druid/Pagan Lectio

Julie Bond

Lectio Divina is a form of slow, deliberate reading of a sacred text which is particularly associated with Christian monastic practice. *Lectio Divina* was originally a purely monastic form of prayer and was used very little outside the monasteries. It was a particular type of reading and was different from the scholastic-type reading which was done more to find information than for purely spiritual purposes. The dogmatic Constitution *Dei Verbum* (The Word of God) appeared in the Second Vatican Council and in this Constitution the practice of *Lectio* was recommended for lay people. This has led to it being a much more widely known and used form of prayer in the wider Christian community. So, what is it?

Lectio = to read
Divina = something holy/sacred

Lectio Divina is a slow meditative reading of something sacred. It is a form of reading more for inspiration than for information. There is no aim to read a lot or accumulate a lot of notes. It is simply done for its own sake, without specific goals in mind. It is perfectly possible to work with the same passage repeatedly over long periods of time.

Generally, Christians will use The Bible for *Lectio*, as they see this as the Word of God. They also see Jesus as the Word, suggesting that "words" don't always have to be written down on a page. This thought led me on to an interesting question: "What is a Druid/Pagan's 'Holy Book'?"

It was a question I was frequently asked during my work as a Pagan Prison Chaplain and my answer often perplexed the questioner. My answer was "Nature is our Holy Book."

Pursuing this line of thought I came to the realization that everything within the natural world can be seen as "words." In developing a Druid/Pagan version of *Lectio Divina* I took the physical creation to be the Gods' words, and so worked with physical objects such as stones, shells, leaves, and twigs, as the "words" of creation's 'text.'

For Christians, God is seen as being present in their sacred scriptures, The Bible, which is why the Bible is the traditional work they use for *Lectio*. I'm not sure it works so well with other scriptures as the Bible is seen as the Word of God and Lectio is seen very much as an encounter with God. For Druids/Pagans, we see the Divine (however we choose to term it) as being present in the natural world, so Nature seemed to me to be the best "book" for *Druid Lectio*. It is constantly changing, always with us, and we are part of it.

The Four Stages of *Lectio Divina*

There are four classic stages in *Lectio Divina*: *Lectio* (reading), *Meditatio* (Meditation), *Oratio* (prayer), *Contemplatio* (Contemplation).

Lectio was first put into these four stages by Guigo II, a Carthusian monk, in the twelfth century. A quote from his book, *The Ladder of Four Rungs*, gives a neat summary of these stages:

"Reading is busily looking on Holy Scripture with all one's will and wit. Meditation is a studious in searching to know what was before concealed through desiring proper skill. Prayer is a devout desiring of the heart to get what is good and avoid what is evil. Contemplation is a lifting up of the heart to God, tasting somewhat of the heavenly sweetness and savor."

Another way to think of these stages could be:

"Reading seeks, meditation finds, prayer asks, contemplation feels."

Or:

"Reading puts, as it were, whole food into your mouth; meditation chews it and breaks it down; prayer finds its savour; contemplation is the sweetness that so delights and savours."

A further way of seeing the Four Stages is: Read, Reflect, Respond, Rest. Some people have seen a link with the Jungian psychological principles;

Sensing – (Read)
Thinking – (Meditate)
Intuiting – (Pray)
Feeling – (Contemplate)

The four stages can flow together smoothly once you get used to the method; in particular I find stages two and three can swirl together.

At the beginning it is a good idea to spend a set amount of time on each stage. Five minutes is a good idea to start with for each stage, as this is easiest to time with a clock or watch.

The following descriptions of the various stages are how I have adapted the existing method of *Lectio Divina* to work with the natural world and natural objects and so using Nature as the Holy Book rather than using a written text. (This is slightly different from the way Christians would work with the Bible.)

I have often done this type of *Lectio* outside and simply picked up something nearby to work with. It doesn't have to be anything stunning to look at; small twigs, stones, pieces of bark, withered leaves, will all work well. It can be really amazing what comes up when working with seemingly "insignificant" things.

Stage of Reading: Looking at the object, not forming any thoughts about it yet, sharing space with it, being aware of it. Think of it as a quieting of the heart. Begin by opening a space within; perhaps this can be seen as more of a calming and a centering. Keep exploring the object. The exploring itself, the interaction, is seen as being transformative.

Stage of Meditation: This concentrates on exploring the object with the senses, allowing discursive, descriptive thoughts to arise, examining the object. (For the early Christian monastics "meditation" meant repeating the words of scripture until they were inscribed on the memory.) Meditation was not so much about "remembering" but more a "thinking about." "Re-membering," a "bringing back together," I would put more in the contemplation stage.

Stage of Prayer: What you feel drawn to say to God/Goddess/ the Divine about the object; any prayer that arises as you examine the object. It can be thanks-giving, petitionary, any kind of prayer which you feel called to bring. The prayer stage is our "response" to what is "said" to us, to what we "hear." "Let our hearts speak to God." At times this has been seen as being more devotional and less petitionary.

Stage of Contemplation: This is almost a return to a similar place as at the beginning of *Lectio,* but at a further turn of the spiral. Contemplation in this sense is about peace, rest. Don't get too hung up on technical definitions of contemplation and what it is or isn't. Rest with the object; let it soak into you. Contemplation is a resting in the presence of the Divine, the idea of deep calling to deep. There can be a sense of becoming aware of yourself and the object as parts of a great oneness, of your edges softening, a feeling of peace, "all is well."

You can have periods of mental silence within all these stages; there is no need to be rushing or struggling to come up with prayers/thoughts etc. This mental silence can help to bring a feeling of spaciousness.

At the close of a session of *Lectio* you can, with thanks, put the object back into the natural world if you are outside and have picked it up there. The feeling is that it returns to the natural world filled with your prayer. It is there to work with again at some time, if you wish. It is also there for anyone else to work with too. There are so many of these 'words;' we will never exhaust the text of creation. There is always more to learn about it, ourselves, and each other. Of course, this type of *Lectio* can be done indoors too, perhaps with a natural object from your shrine or altar which you then replace afterwards, or with an object you have brought indoors for the purpose. You could then place the object on your shrine or altar to work with again at some time, or take it back outside to return it to the natural world.

Working with this form of *Lectio* regularly can bring a strengthening of the feeling of being within the holy book of creation, particularly when out in the natural world.

A view of a landscape could also be used for this type of *Lectio*. This can be very powerful as one can feel oneself as part of that landscape.

It isn't important to always know what is happening in one's practice of *Lectio*. It is more important to simply do it and not be worrying about whether you are doing it 'well' or 'right' or not. There probably isn't a 'right' way to do *Lectio* anyway. It is particularly important to remember that *Lectio* is a way of prayer; waiting and listening are very important, as is attention. There is also the aim of carrying the fruits of your *Lectio* with you all day, of continuing to be nourished by them.

Chapter 7

On the Custody of the Eyes

Rebecca Korvo

There's a longstanding tendency in contemporary Pagan/ polytheist religions to reject everything that can possibly be associated with monotheism (particularly, in the West, Christianity). There is, of course, plenty of justification for this attitude, whether in historical grievances such as forced conversion and cultural genocide, or more personal and familial wounds. But taken too far it can lead to the rejection of basic tools of religious practice. There are Pagans who dismiss the very idea of prayer, who proudly declare they never kneel to their gods, who react with horror to the suggestion that sacrifice may be a necessary part of spiritual growth (the very first time I came across the idea of Pagan monasticism, it was a question on a forum whether anyone had heard of such a thing, and while there were a couple of polite replies, most of them were variations on "no one had better ask me to give up sex, hur hur!"). It bears remembering that the early Christians were not shy about co-opting the useful parts of the ancient paganisms for their own use, whether it be building churches on the sites of former temples or swiping a god or two and turning Them into saints, and, given that Christianity has two millennia of tradition to winnow through, it seems wasteful to dismiss all of their technology of the sacred out of hand.

That said, "custody of the eyes," or *custodia oculorum*, would no doubt seem a strange candidate for reclamation. Mainly taught as a shield in the struggle against lust, it was also enjoined on monastics, nuns in particular, to encourage modesty and humility—all of which sounds about as life-denying and world-despising as anything monotheism has devised. And yet, there is an important truth at the root of the practice: that we choose what we pay attention to, and by that starve or feed ourselves spiritually.

Every weekday, I walk three blocks through downtown between the light rail station and my workplace. Along the route are islands of nature both planned and volunteer: plantings of trees and flowers, the weedy margins of a surface parking lot, a garden of rose bushes, a reflecting pool. I have seen, in my short walks, such wonders as the rising and setting moon; sundogs and solar pillars; bees (honey, bumble, and wild), butterflies and large, lovely moths; rabbits; peregrines; a pair of mallard ducks with their ducklings; and, most surprising of all, a lone wild turkey. In all the time I've traveled that path, only once has anyone stopped to ask what I was looking at. Everyone else? They are, to a person, fixated on their smartphones, oblivious to each other much less to the hidden life around them. I often wonder, had I stopped one of them and pointed out the young rabbit in the rose thicket, if they would have been interested in the least, or shrugged (if not sneered) and strode on to get across the street before the light changed?

Another story: for several weeks last summer, a road crew was tearing up and replacing the pavement along a section of street. One day, while waiting to cross, I looked — really looked — at the layers of asphalt, concrete and brick that covered the dirt below, and suddenly understood that the whole edifice of the city, reaching so impressively high into the sky, was nothing but a thin shell over the soil and stone that had been there since the continent was formed, and that the moment humanity ceased frantically patching and repairing that shell, Nature would insinuate herself into every tiny crack and shatter it. For days after that, I saw not only the present-day city, but the land as it had been before the city rose, and the land as it will be after the city falls, layered like the transparencies in an anatomy book.

These anecdotes, I hope, illustrate the positive use of *custodia oculorum*. It is a practice of double vision, moving through the human world while being always aware of the vibrantly living worlds of Nature and Spirit, which intersect with and infuse the manmade landscape with meaning, with power, and with grace. Even though such observance will sometimes reveal tragedies, such as the crow-devoured baby rabbit I found in an overgrown lot, it still fosters a sense of reverence and connection (and, often, a child's delight in secret knowledge).

While forming my practice, I concentrated entirely upon that positive use of seeing the hidden and the ignored. The idea of *averting* my eyes did not occur. Often, I was enjoined to witness things I would prefer not to see, such the corpse of a sparrow being tossed like a toy by a young hawk, with the clear message, "This too is the Nature you seek to honor." Nonetheless, as I deepened in my polytheism, I found myself naturally curbing my attention and choosing not to view certain things.

The first change was in my tolerance for violence-as-entertainment. I had never been a fan of gruesome horror films, but the increasingly explicit depictions of rape, torture, and mutilation even on network television unsettled me. I found them repellent, not just on the visceral level, but in that I sensed my thoughts and emotions being manipulated: spectacle substituting for character development, action papering over illogical plots, and all in service of luring eyeballs to advertisements. I cut program after program out of my viewing schedule, until I became one of those irritating people who just watch PBS.

As an aside, there was an unexpected bonus to reducing my TV viewing, which was to alter my sense of time. I was annoyed to discover to what extent the television schedule had programmed me to think in blocks of hour, half-hour, and commercial-break increments, and how much more time I had (not seemingly, but in actuality) when that artificial framework was removed. Without television setting its own hyperactive pace, evenings structure themselves around a few tasks to be completed or chapters to be read, before ending with natural tiredness (as opposed to forcing oneself to stay awake to finish a show). Ostensibly, of course, streaming allows you to mold your viewing to your schedule rather than the other way around, but episodes are still blocks of time that can be used for very little else, and streaming offers the new temptation to binge-view through the night—or the entire weekend.

Around the same time, I withdrew from social media, though that was less of a principled boycott and more of a defensive flight. In the buildup to and immediate aftermath of the 2016 presidential election, I witnessed a great number of people fall into terror and hysteria. I waited for them to settle down and regroup for a week... a month... a year. Sadly, too many remained locked in a state of obsessive, anxious rage. Not only did social media timelines morph into endless lists of shared and re-shared and re-re-shared political articles, but every conversation was turned in a political direction—no, let me be clearer, no conversation was allowed to happen without it being twisted in a political direction and devolved into a rant about the vileness of certain political figures or social groups. I would leave these conversations tired and on edge, and finally realized they were toxic for me. Just as with TV and movies, I eliminated online friends (and, sadly, a few real-life friends) and whole social media platforms from my mental landscape.

I still read a number of blogs and belong to a couple of forums, but I am careful to seek out lengthier, more thoughtful sources of commentary and news, and to avoid emotionally-manipulative clickbait headlines. What I have found most useful in controlling the panic-mongering of the contemporary news cycle is meditating on the long cycles of history—the waves of economic booms and busts, the constantly swinging pendulum of political power, the rise and fall of nations, empires, and civilizations, all give perspective that seems both in short supply and desperately needed in our historically-illiterate times.

Most importantly of all, I became sensitized to impiety. I knew the historical degradation of polytheism, first by the monotheistic religions (which turned its gods into demons), then later by the social sciences (which labeled it a "primitive" stage of religious development, exceeded in childish superstition only by animism). I had not grasped just how much of pop culture portrays the gods as monsters, or space aliens, or quarreling spoilt children, or dependent on human attention, anything and everything but mighty and virtuous beings worthy of respect and reverence. It was at this point that I discovered the concept of miasma through the polytheist blogosphere, and learned how corrosive ideas, attitudes, and emotional states can be to our relationships with our gods (even more so because our revived traditions are so young and fragmentary, threatened by monotheism on one side and modernity on the other).

It's only a slight exaggeration to say that whatever media I hadn't shut off or closed the covers on for violence, I ended up doing so for profaneness. That, however, was something I had expected I would need to do, in order to cleanse my mind of obtrusive images and attitudes. What I had not expected was to need to leave a subculture that had been home for over 20 years. Science fiction fandom claims to be a welcoming place for Pagans (and, of course, a great many people have come to Paganism by way of fandom), but it is built on and around that same impious literature and media. More, fandom is rife with what Archdruid Emeritus John Michael Greer terms "the civil religion of progress," a belief system that sees scientific development as a linear trajectory taking humanity from savagery in the caves to eternal life among the stars, not so incidentally dethroning and replacing Deity as the highest power in the universe. The New Atheism was on the rise at the time, and the anti-religious (as opposed to the non-religious) were becoming more vocal in previously neutral fannish spaces. Eventually, my discomfort with the casual disregard for spiritual sensibilities grew too strong to be ignored, and I felt it necessary to leave.

Removing sources of impiety and miasma from our lives may feel over-scrupulous, even cultish, reminiscent of the prudes who once burned comic books and rock-and-roll records. It would perhaps be more helpful to think of it as a detox. When one silences the outer voices calling the gods evil, immoral, imaginary, or delusional and creates a zone of peace for devotion to unfold, one becomes more adept at silencing the inner voices whispering that you really are silly, over-imaginative, and most likely crazy. Moreover, freeing the gods from the mental images human culture has made of Them is necessary in order to begin to know Them in Their more profound and multivalent aspects—an early step on the path to Their mysteries.

None of this is to say that political criticism, or pop culture, or even a bit of cathartic simulated violence is innately bad and to be permanently purged. Not even miasma can or should be avoided at all costs. As more than one Hellenic blogger has pointed out, joyful events such as weddings and virtuous, gods-approved acts such as attending to the dead also cause miasma. Nor can one exist in a bubble, safe from having one's beliefs challenged or peace of mind disturbed. However, as polytheists nurturing our traditions and as monastics developing our practices in defiance of a contemptuous world, we need to prioritize our devotional relationships above the trivial and the transitory. If we are to serve the gods, then we need to make mind and soul still and clear, to receive Their messages and to reflect Their light without distortion.

The dual aspects of *custodia oculorum*—the positive and the negative, the seeking out and the turning away—are not just two sides of a coin, they are, in the end, one and the same. Regardless of which form one starts with, inevitably they feed into each other: the negative creating mental space for the positive to fill, attention to the holy and nurturing pushing out the unholy and toxic. *Custodia* is a practice that demands discipline and discernment, but this odd relic of medieval monasticism is surprisingly useful in creating a mental state conducive to devotion and welcoming of the Holy Powers.

Chapter 8

Of Hearth and Shadow

A Contemplative Norse Polytheist and a Fledgling Animist Sanctuary

Danica Swanson

In Praise of Holy Darkness

> *May we hearken to the wisdom and gifts of darkness, rest, and shadow.*
>
> *May we remember to create space for silence, stillness, solitude, and mystery.*
>
> *May we dwell respectfully in states of unknowing and non-doing.*
>
> *May we permit our imagination unfettered freedom in contemplation of the sacred.*
>
> *Praise be to the Holy Powers.*
>
> - Prayer at Black Stone Sanctuary

One misty April day in 2011, a few years after my divorce, a black obsidian scrying stone stamped indelibly into my mind's eye a vision of a monastic retreat. Designed specifically for polytheists and animists with hermit inclinations, the restful and contemplative retreat space included a subterranean shrine room for the Norse huntress deity Skaði, and other design elements paying homage to the Holy Powers. The premises also housed a monastic library, a meditation hut featuring dark ambient and low-frequency drone music, a courtyard "cloister," and a thriving permaculture forest garden laden with coniferous evergreen trees, fungi, and lush moss-covered stones.

"Begin it right here, in the space you've got right now,"

instructed the stone. "You may serve as designer, caretaker, and scribe."

Moved by the detailed vision of building a retreat in honor of the beloved goddess Who helped me survive a nightmarish divorce and an ill-fated intentional community effort, I resolved to build it for Her or die trying. An ancestral force residing deep within my bones and flesh compelled me. But how? Snowed under with post-divorce grief and recession-induced financial desperation, I occupied a tiny seventh-floor live/work studio in the heart of a city building, with no access to land, basement space, or funding.

"You must publicly document the work in writing right from the outset, flaws and all," insisted the stone, as translated into the written word through my intuitive faculties. "Even if it's not yet recognized in an organized way, every monastery must begin somewhere."

At this point I'd considered myself some flavor of polytheistic Pagan since the mid-1990s, and a Heathen since 2004, the year I first met Skaði and began keeping company with Her. Inspired, I consecrated my little studio to Skaði, experimented with head coverings and makeshift nun habits, began teaching myself WordPress, and started a project named after the stone: Black Stone Sanctuary (previously known as The Black Stone Hermitage). The Sanctuary serves as both a physical location and a concept through which I extend artistic and religious community services. I've developed the online and in-person aspects of the Sanctuary roughly in parallel.

With the help of collaborators and supporters from my local Heathen group, I transformed the Sanctuary's studio space into a mini-retreat, and began hosting visitors for incubation retreats. Eventually I settled on what to call the Sanctuary: "a contemplative dark incubation retreat inspired by animist pre-Christian Norse and Germanic religious and folk traditions." In the intervening years I also carried out several public outreach projects, including hosting a hotel shrine room for Skaði at a polytheist conference, and serving as an administrator of online discussion groups for polytheist monastics.

When the Sanctuary finds a new home with a suitable subterranean space, the next phase of its religious outreach and service work will commence.

Of Hearth: Discerning a Calling

Perhaps my monastic discernment process began in earnest in 1992, when a psilocybin mushroom initiated me in my college dorm room. The mushroom informed me that I'd been claimed. Or something like that. I did not speak mushroom-ese and had no translator, so many years passed before I began to understand.

Or maybe it began with the spirit lover who visited me several times in 1988, long before I learned that there were nuns who lived as "brides of Christ" and meant it literally: that they interacted with divine forces *that* way. Sleep paralysis? Apparitions? Incubus, elf, or mare visits? Maybe. Maybe not. In any case, that visceral force identified me as a vessel.

Whatever the origin, it took me over two decades to assemble enough pieces of the puzzle to reveal a clear pattern. Monastic discernment can be difficult for animists, it turns out, when one must discern such an abstruse vocation without the grounding of existing models.

Mystical visions aside, at some point my daily habits ticked an increasing number of boxes fitting a classic monastic profile. Contented with solitude. Avowed bibliophile. Writer. Introvert. Meditator. Non-drinker, on-smoker. Non-parent. Meticulously clean and organized hearth-tender and homebody, with little interest in shopping, fashion, cars, sports, parties, or media entertainment.

I also bonded viscerally and emotionally with certain buildings - especially small homes with basements - on levels

I struggled to articulate. Perhaps if a framework of monastic discernment for animists had been a thing, I might have interpreted my early affinity for basements, caves, dark closets, tents, blanket forts, and other enclosed spaces as another way my hermit calling tried to get my attention. Not until 2006, when I discovered online writings by Pagan monastics, did I connect the dots.

It was the power of limits, though, that served as the final clincher. I'd been a libertine in my youth, so the sense of liberation I discovered through embracing monastic limits in middle age took me by surprise. When I realized solitude and monastic service had become vastly more important and nourishing to me than romance, for example, I stopped dating. (I made a vow to Skaði: if She wanted me partnered, She'd have to do the work of getting our paths to cross. Barring that, I'd gladly stay single. To this day, that vow stands.)

My changing tastes in clothing fit the monastic pattern, too: long tunics, floor-length skirts, abayas, head wraps. Limiting my wardrobe to nun-like clothing and covering my body from head to toe stirred a deep sense of fulfillment in ways I'd never dreamed it could. These experiments drove home for me a paradoxical truth of monasticism: structure can be liberating.

Religious callings often make themselves known through gifts or talents. In my case, two overlapping spheres are involved: wordsmithing and arranging interior dwelling spaces in emotionally engaging ways. I create and care for contemplative spaces and atmospheres, both figurative and literal. As an animist, I approach homes as beings with agency, and work with them to construct atmospheres that speak to aspects of the human animal that are inaccessible through the intellect alone.

If polytheistic monasticism were well-established with scripted roles, I'd serve as scribe and sacristan, holding responsibility for designing, creating, and documenting the atmosphere of the worship environment. I'd select, arrange, and maintain liturgical vessels, incense, shrine accoutrements, fabrics, curtains, lighting, furnishings, vestments, and other supplies. I'd also work closely with musicians and sound designers to customize the aural aspects of the worship space.

About the Sanctuary

Black Stone Sanctuary seems to serve as a magnet for obscure Ásynjur (goddesses), and is consecrated into Their service. We honor Skaði, Frigg and Her Court (Handmaidens), Menglöð, and the Maidens of Lyfjaberg. Morðguð occasionally makes an appearance. More recently, Nótt and Njörun paid the Sanctuary a first visit in conjunction with our dark moon incubation retreats. We also pay respects and make service offerings to many other non-human beings of the Pacific Northwest, including stones, conifers, and fungi. We work with literal black touchstones as well as metaphorical touchstones, translating their guidance into service within ongoing relationships of reciprocity.

Monastic practice at the Sanctuary includes meditation, *lectio divina*, restorative yoga, ascetic and aesthetic practices, deep listening facilitated by dark ambient and drone music, shrine tending, tea rituals, and making aromatic blends with foraged materials from conifers such as Douglas Fir and Western Redcedar. Liturgical development at the Sanctuary includes chant, hymn, call-and-response, and spoken prayer (including prayer beads). One of our chant projects involves an attempt to learn all 66 stanzas of Sveinbjörn Beinteinsson's chanting of the Völuspá.[1]

We are collecting inspiration for planning our monastic habits. Religious clothing helps us maintain demarcations from secular culture, demonstrate respect for the Holy Powers we serve, and reinforce our commitment to service.

The Sanctuary also follows a short monastic rule: "Follow the Ways of Non-Contrivance." Delivered in dreams and confirmed repeatedly through prayer and meditation, the rule calls forth many questions. It suggests multiple layers of meaning and paradox, yet provides few clear answers. For starters, we interpret it as an edict to develop the monastic structures in modular, emergent, decentralized, bottom-up ways rather than impose them through contrivance or centralized top-down planning. At this early stage the rule exists as a single sentence; with time it may expand. In animist terms, following the ways of non-contrivance means listening attentively to the persons who inspire the Sanctuary's work, and using this guidance to pull together various elements until patterns emerge.

Of Shadow: Sacred Endarkenment and Animism

"The highest and best in human beings is subtle, mysterious, and tied directly to the shadows. Life is both unbearably cruel and devastatingly sweet, often at the same time." - Karin L. Burke, The Yoga of Darkness[2]

The Sanctuary aims to cultivate animist and ecocentric perceptual capacities that have been de-legitimized and suppressed through enculturation. Animism, as a world-accepting view based in relationships of mutuality and reciprocity with human and non-human beings, serves as the foundation that shapes our monastic practices.

Within this context, we use the neologism *sacred endarkenment* to denote the principles and practices of holding respectful space for beings and places of holy darkness, both literal and metaphorical. While darkness is often associated with fear, evil, ignorance, destruction, and negativity, we honor and inhabit darkness as a refuge - a gateway to deeper layers of insight, slower rhythms of life, and direct religious experience. Niðhogg lurks at the roots of Yggdrasil, reminding us that compost, rot, death, ashes, and decay generate new life, and are just as sacred as growth, joy, and light. Darkness and shade nurture thriving, resilient ecosystems with lush fungi and verdant mosses.

Animism does not hold intellectual knowledge as inherently superior to other ways of knowing. Nor does it sanctify light over darkness. Contemplative practice for animists, then, involves learning in relational, experiential, nonverbal ways through accumulated intelligence and ancestral memories held in our bodies and the body of Jorð. Books or maps are of limited use. To communicate effectively with spirits of place, we must trust in our capacities for imagination, instinct, discernment, and feeling.

Toward that end, monastics can engage with spaces of holy darkness deliberately, as a way to connect with spirits and the taproot of being. In this way we are sometimes reminded that what we need most often comes to us unbidden, quite apart from what we consciously want and what we seek through deliberate effort. As I learned in my early initiation-by-fungi, certain beings of shadow may impart animist wisdom through mystical encounters with the Void, the Abyss, and other vast formless sources of creation. Darkness can sometimes be fearful and harrowing, yet she can also be kindly, safe, and accepting - often at the same time. Retreating into darkness may present a challenge for those of us weaned on a steady diet of colonialist metaphors of light and ascension. But she can offer deep rest, succor, and the comfort of concealment until seeds have germinated and gathered enough strength to support growth.

While sacred endarkenment involves surrender, it does not involve passivity or giving up. It's a deepening humility and acceptance of our rule. It's a sense of trust that following ways of non-contrivance can reveal truths that would not be found any other way.

A related phrase we often use in its myriad layers of meaning is *shadow work*. In the Jungian sense, shadow work addresses repressed, hidden, disowned, or denied parts of human nature.

Ivan Illich uses shadow work to call attention to the many forms of unwaged toil that prop up waged work.[3] The Sanctuary employs the phrase in these ways and more.

While polytheists do not proselytize, if the Sanctuary were entreated to preach the "gospel" of anything, our sermons would center on developing societies and cultures that respect and honor holy darkness in its many forms. We seek to provide a corrective balancing measure to the overemphasis on light, transcendence, and ascension.

Sacred endarkenment can also denote respect for the alchemical wisdom contained within "negative" emotions. Catherine MacCoun writes in *On Becoming An Alchemist* that the best way to transmute anything is to encourage it to be fully *as it is*.[4] *Genuine* positivity, for example - as opposed to the admonitions we internalize through faux positivity culture - emerges as embodied experience. The door to true emotional positivity opens only when we allow challenging emotions the opportunity to move through the body unimpeded, and this process begins with acknowledging pain that we hold there. Surrendering our efforts to repress and control allows emotions to be fully *as they are*, which is a prerequisite for full integration. "What we resist, persists" is especially true of emotions, and it's among the many paradoxical truths of animist monasticism.

Cultivating respect for darkness in all its forms entreats us to exercise care with the language surrounding these concepts. We avoid using "light" as a synonym for "good" and "dark" as a synonym for "bad," for example, and any similar constructions. The same goes for "higher" and "lower." Praying to multiple "lower powers" or underworld beings may not ever gain as much cultural traction as praying to a singular "higher power" in a monotheist-dominant culture obsessed with ascension. Nonetheless, animists know that deep truth resides in dark places, and we ignore or suppress it to our own peril.

Dwelling in spaces of shadow, rest, receptivity, and surrender can lead us to hidden sources of power, nourishment, and sustenance. Our culture greatly needs to reclaim the wisdom of emergence and sacred endarkenment. Perhaps this is why it appears in the zeitgeist as well as in the Sanctuary's work to build an animist monastic practice from the ground up.

One of our guiding maxims for developing an animist monastery is that the best in humans is tied to the shadows.

Offerings of Shadow: Incubation Sanctuaries

Animists relate to places, including buildings, as beings that deserve care and respect. Through our Black Tent Temple Project, the Sanctuary explores modern incubation practices for monastic use in polytheist-animist contexts. Over time, places accumulate emotional and spiritual resonance through recurrent patterns of use, including combinations of visual, auditory, spatial, architectural, and olfactory cues. Using principles of sacred endarkenment, these elements can be combined to create atmospheres that meet needs that often go unfulfilled in a culture obsessed with productivity and control. The Sanctuary explores the emotional resonance of endarkened spaces through ascetic and aesthetic practices. Our Black Tent Temple space combines elements of both sensory deprivation and sensory engagement.

From a historical perspective, incubation refers to a ritual practice of lying down - usually within a subterranean space of some sort - and sleeping or entering a liminal state that enables divinatory or therapeutic dreams and visions to emerge through forces inaccessible via waking awareness. Key to this practice is the insight that the forces engaged in these contexts cannot be controlled or directed in any way; they can only be allowed, and they only show up when they are ready. Incubation spaces rely on co-creation efforts between caretaker and space. When the caretaker sets up the appropriate conditions, the architecture and design of the space itself may handle much of the necessary work.

At the Sanctuary we simply create the space, as best we can, and get out of the way so the various beings who attend to the retreatants' needs can do their thing. Since the space itself often does a larger share of the work, there's less pressure on us to act as directors. The spiritual-material power available in these contexts results from acknowledging our limits, releasing all forms of subtle coercion and effort, and accepting beings *as they are* rather than trying to make them over into something else.

We shape the walls of our retreat spaces to resemble cave-like features using felt lining, thick velvet curtains, or other soft sound-absorbing material that speaks to the nesting instinct. We design the spaces to provide respite from the cacophony of everyday life, encourage quietude and restfulness, and engage the intelligence of the enteric nervous system more than the much-vaunted intellect.

Well-designed endarkened incubation spaces offer many benefits that facilitate animist contemplative practice. They can evoke a primal sense of being deeply held, supported, and safely nestled within a dark and nourishing cocoon. They can kindle emotional release and a sense of being suspended in timelessness. They can help us realign with animism by drawing attention to how much our possibilities are shaped and constrained by our environment, inviting us to question narratives that stress the importance of being "self-supporting." They can also help remind us of the underground beings and forces at many levels that support us, including geomantic forces, telluric currents, and chthonic deities.

For the Black Tent Temple Project, we take inspiration from the darkroom retreat movements occurring in both religious and secular contexts. Examples include Tibetan Buddhist dark retreats and restful darkrooms designed according to hygienic principles by Andrew Durham.[5] The rest-as-resistance movement and a growing body of writings on the various meanings and applications of shadow work also provide a wealth of inspiration for the Sanctuary.

We consider deep rest to be an important religious matter for animists. Accordingly, we seek to develop an approach to monasticism informed by Nordic animism, including theologies and philosophies of rest and leisure. Preserving long stretches of unstructured time for rest creates room for unexpected material to be revealed from the shadows. Overloaded schedules change the character and experience of time. In the expansive texture of time experienced in contemplative solitude, by contrast, we preserve space for emergent material.

How might we find restful ways of monastic life as contemplative polytheists-animists? Our theory is that practices of sacred endarkenment, such as responsible design and use of incubation sanctuaries, may represent one step in the right direction.

Challenges

An obvious challenge we face is the lack of precedents for polytheist-animist monasticism. While every religion has mystics and contemplatives who are more drawn to religious community service than conventional career and family structures, polytheist contemplatives currently have no organized spaces to carry out these forms of service. We're attempting to discern and carry out vocations that cannot be reliably and fully reconstructed from ancient practices, so we have few viable choices but to build support structures ourselves and/or somehow tap into the existing infrastructure of other religions.

Another major consideration involves fundamental differences in worldviews. Polytheist-animist ˙ worldviews represent a radical departure from the dominant secular and monotheistic worldviews. Even interfaith efforts like New Monasticism can replicate many of the foundational assumptions of monotheism. Interfaith work can prove untenable for some polytheists, as many interfaith approaches are still structured according to monotheistic principles. For one thing, even the *name* marginalizes traditions that may place more emphasis on praxis than they do on faith or belief.

Furthermore, if the interfaith work contains a subtext of monism, holding that different religions represent paths to the same underlying unity, then polytheists may find ourselves further marginalized before we even begin. So, a major challenge polytheist monastics face is, as Charles Eisenstein writes;

"we must deal with an environment that enforces the old habits, not only through economic and social means, but through a relentless barrage of subtle messaging that takes for granted the very things we are seeking to change."[6]

Such as, for example, the split between "natural" and "supernatural," or referring to deities using only the past tense. These framings advance narratives based on separation, and portray deities not as Holy Powers worthy of respect, but as archaeological and mythological curiosities safely relegated to the past.

Lack of social support for these ventures presents another daunting challenge. "Hard" polytheist theology sometimes meets with snide comments (if it even registers on the radar at all), which takes an emotional toll over time. Even many Heathens internalize the "monotheistic gaze," the cultural narrative that portrays polytheism as something only the ancients believed, and the dismissal of animism as naive superstition. Genuine worship, prayer, genuflection, and earnest devotional practice in animist contexts put us in a vulnerable position. We're marginalized in secular and atheist culture, monotheist religions, much of big-tent Paganism, the ranks of the spiritual-but-not-religious, and many segments of Heathenism. As a result, many of us hesitate to discuss our theologies and monastic practices with nearly anyone.

Monastics in new religious movements also face the challenge of determining what, precisely, differentiates monastics from laity. A few examples we've discussed at the Sanctuary include:

- Discerning monasticism as a primary vocation and a long-term calling to religious service.
- Consistently conducting one's life according to principles of a monastic Rule.
- Taking monastic vows before one's peers and the Holy Powers.
- Asceticism: abstaining from certain activities or life choices (substances, media entertainment, etc.) for the sake of one's spiritual practice.
- Clothing that demarcates the monastic from non-monastics, identifying them as part of a religious order (e.g., regularly wearing a habit).
- Ordered, repetitive religious practice thoroughly integrated into one's daily habits and living situation. Examples: A set liturgical routine marking the daily hours. Dedicating and consecrating a physical space solely to monastic practice. "Making the rounds" with steady and structured rhythms of prayer, rest, study, worship, meditation, contemplation, chant, music, and work.

We don't view any of these as necessarily definitive in and of themselves; it's the combination of them all, or most of them, that differentiates a polytheist monastic from a non-monastic. While it's perfectly appropriate for each monastic group to maintain its own set of standards, we trust that eventually some general themes will emerge to clarify boundaries demarcating monastics from non-monastics.

The Future of Polytheist-Animist Monasticism

Despite the above challenges, there is reason for optimism about the future of monastic endeavors in our communities. The first wave of polytheists practicing monasticism, as far as I know, began with the formation of the Maetreum of Cybele, founded in 1997.[7] To this day the Maetreum remains the only legally recognized polytheist Pagan convent in the U.S. Many other Pagan and polytheistic monastic endeavors have launched since then, not all of which engage in public outreach. Some are legally incorporated as churches, if not explicitly identified as monasteries. One of the most well-known is the Order of the Horae associated with the Church of Asphodel, publishers of the Pagan Book of Hours. This church maintains a collection of online shrines for many Norse deities.[8]

Deities from many traditions seem to be calling modern monastics to service, and if the uptick in interest the Sanctuary has seen is any indication, the coming years will bring many more experimental monastic endeavors. Once the necessary legal, financial, and physical infrastructure is established and word gets out about it, well-managed polytheist monasteries will likely attract a great deal of interest.

Black Stone Sanctuary hosted the first regional meeting of Pacific Northwest-based polytheist monastics in 2019, and we field many queries from people drawn to the Norse deities who seek to develop contemplative practices in ways that are not well represented among Heathens at the moment. We'd love to be able to point them to more monastic options.

For monastics aspiring to build physical infrastructure, one promising model involves cooperative ownership of land and buildings with a religion with a larger following, such as Buddhism or progressive Christianity. Some groups are exploring the possibilities of setting up monastic co-housing, planning hermit cottages clustered together in pocket neighborhoods centered around a religious gathering space, repurposing vacant churches and outbuildings, or working with community land trusts. Starting small might enable monastic projects to get started earlier than they could otherwise.

Since Black Stone Sanctuary is in Portland, which has a thriving accessory dwelling unit (ADU) culture, we've considered the possibility of pairing with homeowners interested in building an ADU on the premises for religious purposes. As an audiophile I have a particular interest in the eco-friendly and acoustic properties of hempcrete, so when the Sanctuary finds its new home, I hope to build hempcrete structures to host acoustically enhanced worship and meditation spaces.

The growth in location-independent internet work options is enacting cultural and structural changes that can lend themselves to monastic possibilities. This includes increased options to build monasteries in more affordable areas and integrate paid online work into the rhythms of monastic practice. Right now, I support most of Black Stone Sanctuary's financial needs through my work as a self-employed professional editor working remotely. Since my health conditions make travel difficult, this is a real boon for the Sanctuary. It enables me to spend more time on online outreach and community service than I could otherwise.

Other monastics also use the internet to offer a window into their contemplative practice from a distance, through synchronous distance meditations and offertory services ("virtual church"). Some groups accept petitions and prayer requests from their communities. These practices can strengthen monastic communities without the need for regular travel.

Online platforms enabling direct payments to independent artists from their followers might be fruitfully directed to monastic purposes as well. Live-streaming platforms enable listeners to pay musicians directly for online concerts, for example. Perhaps nuns and monks chanting the Völuspá or singing hymns could partner with musicians, videographers, and other professionals to bring monastic arts to their communities. Meditation or sacred dance instructors might offer courses through platforms such as Teachable. Musicians might release albums on Bandcamp. Writers might publish newsletters on platforms such as Substack, as we do for Black Stone Sanctuary. Monastics with the requisite skills have more options than ever before for online outreach. What will the second wave of polytheist-animist monastic ventures be like? I look forward to finding out.

Endnotes

1 NorseTube, Völuspá by Sveinbjörn Beinteinsson, 2012. https://www.youtube.com/watch?v=xisBERxHJ6g&feature =youtu.be

2 Karin L. Burke, "The Yoga of Darkness." *Return Yoga*, August 21, 2013. https://www.returnyoga.org/blog/rage-fear-sadness-fatigue-and-yoga-the-yoga-of-darkness

3 Ivan Illich, *Shadow Work*. Salem, New Hampshire and London: Marion Boyars, 1981. https://en.wikipedia.org/ wiki/Shadow_work

4 Catherine MacCoun, *On Becoming an Alchemist: A Guide for the Modern Magician*. Trumpeter Books, 2008, p. 241.

5 Chinese Buddhist Encyclopedia," A Western Approach to Tibetan Dark Retreat Meditation," and Andrew Durham, *Hygienic Darkroom Retreat: Profound Rest for the Self-Healing Psyche*. https://darkroomretreat.com/ http://www.chinabuddhismencyclopedia.com/en/index. php/A_Western_Approach_to_Tibetan_Dark_Retreat_ Meditation

6 Charles Eisenstein, *The More Beautiful World Our Hearts Know is Possible*. Berkeley, CA: North Atlantic Books, p. 109. https://charleseisenstein.org/books/the-more-beautiful-world-our-hearts-know-is-possible/

7   Maetreum of Cybele. https://www.gallae.com/
8   Church of Asphodel and Order of the Horae. https://www.
     churchofasphodel.org/
     https://www.paganbookofhours.org/horae/monasticfaq.
     html

Chapter 9

Toward the Hermitage of the Heart

John Michael Greer

What meaningful form could the traditions of monasticism take in today's world—in particular, for participants in the nature spirituality of the Druid Revival? That was the question I and the other members of the Grand Grove of the Ancient Order of Druids in America (AODA) began to explore more than a decade ago. I'd like to devote a few pages here to explaining how those explorations proceeded and what came out of them, for reasons that I'll explain a little later on.

Some discussion of the background will probably be necessary to make sense of what follows, since the Druid Revival is not your common or garden variety Neopagan movement— strictly speaking, it's not Neopagan at all—and AODA is decidedly quirky even by Druid Revival standards. The Druid Revival emerged in Britain back in the eighteenth century as small groups of people became dissatisfied with the spiritual options on offer in their culture. Faced with a Hobson's choice between dogmatic Protestant Christianity and equally dogmatic scientific materialism, they invented a third option: a nature-centered spirituality inspired partly by what little was known about the ancient Druids, partly by Western esoteric teachings, and partly by the great spiritual traditions of Asia, which were beginning to filter into Europe in those same years.

The resulting movement doesn't fit most of the conventional categories of today's spirituality. Even so basic a question as how many deities are worshiped, if any—many? Two? One? None? —has no single answer in Druid Revival traditions, and most of the surviving Druid Revival organizations find it easy to make room for all these options and more. Nor is Christianity, the *bête noir* of so many alternative traditions these days, excluded from the mix; at a typical Druid Revival ritual, you can expect to find Christian Druids, Neopagan Druids, polytheist Druids, pantheist Druids, animist Druids, and Druids who aren't quite sure what if anything they believe, all standing in a circle together and sharing the same rituals.

If that sounds eccentric, it should. The Druid Revival is an oddity among today's nature-centered spiritual movements. It isn't descended from the ancient Druids, or from any other romantic ancient tradition, and its members are by and large not greatly interested in reconstructing practices from ancient sources; it has its own traditions, created and refined over the three hundred years of its history, which serve it well. In many ways, it's best understood as an indigenous nature religion of modern Anglo-American culture.

And AODA? It was founded in Boston in 1912 by a group of American Freemasons, who obtained a charter for the purpose from a British Druid organization. Never particularly large or particularly public, it's one of thousands of small to mid-sized spiritual groups that have provided alternatives to the mainstream religions in American life since Colonial times. When I joined it in 2003, it was nearly extinct, with fewer than a dozen members, none but me under retirement age. Shortly after joining, I was asked to become a member of the Grand Grove, with the title of Archdruid of Air; three months later I found myself with the resplendent title of Grand Archdruid of the Grand Grove of the Ancient Order of Druids in America. My job was to apply shock paddles to the prostrate body of the order and get it on its feet, and that task occupied the next twelve years of my life.

That project was made even more interesting than it otherwise would be because the one active AODA grove in the order's declining years was located in and around Boulder, CO, and ended up first sharing members and then effectively merging with several other small occult and alternative-spirituality groups active in the same area. Along with the initiations, ordinations, and empowerments of a third-degree member and archdruid of AODA, as a result, I was also initiated into each of these other traditions — the Modern Order of Essenes, the Order of Spiritual Alchemy, the Holy Order of the Golden Dawn, and the Universal Gnostic Church. Those were in no better shape than AODA when I joined, all but one of them was effectively defunct by the time AODA was more or less back on its feet, and the last went out of existence a few years ago, finding the fate AODA narrowly escaped.

The Universal Gnosis

It was in 2008 that the idea of dusting off some of the other traditions we'd inherited along with AODA was first brought up for discussion in the Grand Grove — the seven-member group tasked, under the order's constitution, with managing AODA's affairs. By then we'd established a website, an email list, and a study program, and brought in a few hundred members. A handful of local groves and study groups had been established, and I'd published two books, *The Druidry Handbook* and *The Druid Magic Handbook*, which presented AODA's quirky take on Druid Revival spirituality to a mostly baffled world. Some of the order's members were interested in a more specifically religious, sacramental dimension to Druidry, and so our attention turned to the Universal Gnostic Church (UGC), one of the alternative groups mentioned above.

The UGC had its own odd history. It was founded in 1951 by three Universalist ministers, who objected to the proposed merger with the Unitarians then being explored by the rest of the Universalist Church. The founders of the UGC were consecrated as bishops in one of the French Gnostic lineages — we still haven't been able to identify which one — and launched itself as an independent church. (A later UGC presiding archbishop, John Gilbert, was consecrated by Archbishop Herman A. Spruit of the Church of Antioch and consecrated all the other UGC bishops to regularize the UGC's claim to apostolic succession.) The UGC never had more than a handful of congregations, but one of the founding bishops, Matthew Shaw, moved to Boulder in 1972 and became a member of AODA. In 1978 Shaw became the fourth Grand Archdruid of AODA, and established the tradition by which all AODA archdruids are consecrated *ex officio* as bishops in the UGC.

Under Archbishop Shaw, the UGC also established two other organizations with fascinating possibilities. The Order of the Universal Monk and the Order of the Universal Nun were meant for members of the UGC who wished to take up a monastic life. Since the UGC placed a high value on personal autonomy, a central task of postulants for either of these two orders was that of writing, under the guidance of the bishop who would administer their final vows, the monastic rule they would follow thereafter. As far as any of us could find out, these two orders were defunct by the time we began crafting our own monasticism—though there may still be members of each of them somewhere in the world, still following their self-designed rules—but we decided the ideas behind these two orders had a great deal to offer our eccentric Druid order and its equally eccentric members.

Monasticism generally offered a way around one of the least productive habits of the Neopagan movement—the habit of assuming, usually without thinking much about it, that the idiosyncratic habits and notions of mainstream American Protestant Christianity are by definition the way religion is or ought to be. To see this oddity of thought in full flower, watch what happens when a Neopagan group decides that it wants to have ordained ministers. Nearly always—no matter how irrelevant these things may be to the traditions of the group in question—the conversation veers at once toward paid clergy who hold weekly services for lay congregations, officiate at weddings and funerals, and generally tell everyone else what to do in matters of faith, morals, and (as often as not) politics.

. None of these functions are relevant to AODA, or to the Druid Revival more generally; what's more, most of it is equally antithetical to the traditional values of the UGC. Most groups in the Druid Revival tradition have no clergy at all, the few that do have clergy don't permit that status to become a moneymaking opportunity, and people who take part in a Druid Revival ritual are active participants, not passive members of a congregation. As for letting clergy tell them how to live their lives—or how to cast their ballots—a great many people who come to Druidry from other faiths are specifically interested in getting away from that sort of covert authoritarianism, and want a spirituality that affirms individual autonomy rather than demanding blind obedience.

In the UGC, in turn, personal spiritual experience is the heart of the Universal Gnosis, and the role of UGC clergy was always that of facilitators, helping individuals to find and follow their own gnosis. We discussed this on the Grand Grove email list before taking it to the membership, and explained these points in detail to our members—and yet, with maddening predictability, the moment the discussion got under way, some members of the order immediately redefined everything we'd said in terms of generic Protestant religious practice, and all too obviously aspired to clergy status so they could perform weddings, get paid to hold services for congregations, and claim unearned authority to tell other people what to do. We actually had people try to insist that prospective AODA clergy should be required to get a M.Div. degree from a seminary—a proposal that would have turned AODA into a carbon copy of the institutions so many of its members had fled in dismay or disgust.

That was how the concept of monasticism entered our discussions, as a way to define what our tradition had to offer and foreclose certain predictable stupidities—when you say "monk" or "nun," in effect, you short-circuit the mental hiccup that makes so many people identify the concept of "clergy" solely with the role filled by Parson Brown of the local Methodist Church. Once we began to explore the idea of monasticism, though, it took on a life of its own, as the members of the Grand Grove realized what it could mean to have a monastic form of spirituality available as an option for members of AODA who took the order's traditions and practices seriously. In early 2010, after extensive discussions, the Grand Grove decided to go ahead with the explorations then in process, and Archdruid of Water Sara Greer became the order's point person for what we then called "the monasticism project."

The Rule of Awen

Several possibilities went out the window early on. We considered and quickly discarded the idea of trying to found a brick-and-mortar monastery, partly because we didn't have the money, partly because we'd witnessed other spiritual organizations dragged down to collapse by the costs of maintaining real estate, and partly because several of us had witnessed attempts at group living arrangements in the Neopagan and occult scenes already and knew that as a rule, the first people who volunteer for such projects are the last people anyone else should ever have to try to live with. We considered and then dismissed the option of inserting the monastic structure into the existing AODA study program, and decided to give it an independent organization. We also explored and discarded the idea of having a detailed monastic rule for all to follow—that was, we all felt, antithetical to the principles of the AODA and the UGC alike. It was in the wake of those conversations that the concept of Awen moved toward the center of our reflections.

Awen is a Welsh word with no exact English equivalent. It means inspiration and the spirit of inspiration, the poet's muse, the unseen influence that guides and directs. Early on in the Druid Revival it became a core concept, and Revival teachings came to see each soul as having its own distinct Awen, a unique inspiration and guiding spirit that is also the soul's destiny. If you want a simple definition of the point and purpose of Druidry in the Revival traditions, "finding and following your Awen" is about as close as you can come. The resonance between that and the self-created monastic rule of the Orders of the Universal Monk and Nun was obvious. Over a long series of discussions, tempered with a lot of meditation, we settled on "find and follow your own Awen" as the basic principle behind the rule of our incipient monastic tradition—the Rule of Awen, as we called it.

These reflections also inspired the one firm prohibition we made part of our monastic rule: no one following that rule can claim religious or moral authority over any other person. To take seriously the idea that every person has a unique Awen, an inspiration and a destiny that is not identical to anyone else's, is to surrender any claim to have a right to tell anyone else what to do. That principle, we decided, needed to apply to the leadership of the monastic organization as well; if a member violated the prohibition, they would not be told to stop—but they would be asked to resign or, if necessary, expelled from the organization and allowed to follow their inspiration along some other path.

In the same way, and for some of the same reasons, we decided to make a shared ritual practice central to the monastic path we were creating. As noted below, it took some time and effort to come up with a ritual that could be worked by people irrespective of the deities or impersonal powers they revere, but some common focus of practice was clearly called for, to provide a nucleus of shared experience and spiritual power on which participants could draw. Here again, we rejected the idea that the organization should require anyone to practice the shared ritual, but we agreed that those whose Awen did not lead them to commit to that practice would be helped to find some other path for their spiritual needs outside our monastic framework.

Those decisions helped us clear a way through certain other perplexities. Since neither the AODA nor the UGC have ever claimed to be the only valid spiritual path, it became clear to us that we could define certain teachings and practices as central to our new monasticism, and offer the result as an option for those people who felt called to those teachings and practices, encouraging others to look elsewhere for paths better suited to their personal Awen. The process of teasing out the teachings from the mass of not very systematic lore we inherited, and the even less organized body of material that had been developed by enthusiastic members since the AODA's revival, kept us busy for a while, but we finally settled on three keywords drawn from UGC tradition: "Gnostic," "Universalist," and "Pelagian."

Those are fancy ways of talking about the core themes the UGC has followed from the beginning, and the AODA adopted from the UGC and other sources early in its history. "Gnostic" means that the central theme of the path is based on personal spiritual experience (*gnosis* in Greek), not belief in doctrines handed down by tradition or authority. "Universalist" means the recognition that gnosis is available to all and is present throughout the universe, not restricted to a self-proclaimed spiritual elite. "Pelagian" refers back to a once-famous heresy set in motion by a Celtic monk of late Roman times named Pelagius, who argued that the human soul is responsible for its own fate and can achieve salvation by its own efforts; that was a convenient label for the principles of personal autonomy and individual inspiration we'd already settled on as central themes for our project.

The Hermitage of the Heart

Somewhere in the course of these discussions, we also settled on the basic outer framework of our monastic system: the Hermitage of the Heart. The term came from an exercise two of us had learned years before from an experienced ceremonial magician in Seattle, but the concept took on new dimensions as we tried to make sense of what the Rule of Awen meant when applied to life in the material world. The idea of a hermit—a solitary monastic, as distinct from one who lived with others in a monastery—had obvious relevance to our project, since an order with a thousand members scattered across five continents was unlikely to give rise to large local concentrations of monastics!

The concept of the Hermitage of the Heart was partly a reflection of that reality, and partly a natural outgrowth of the Rule of Awen. The hermits of old followed rules of life they themselves had established; where they lived, how they supported themselves, and what spiritual practices they performed—other than those central to whatever faith they followed—spanned a galaxy of diverse options. What united them was an orientation that put the spiritual realm, as distinct from social or material concerns, at the center of their lives, and a willingness to follow a solitary path and do without the support of fellow practitioners.

We realized at once, though, that the outward solitude of the traditional hermit was by no means a necessity for the path we had in mind. Most people who follow any kind of spiritual path in today's obsessively materialistic society know the kind of solitude that can be experienced in the middle of a crowd of thousands, or in the closest moments of interpersonal contact— the solitude marked off by the gap between the things our culture is willing to include in its vision of reality and the things it rejects. That, we realized, was the solitude that matters for any contemporary monastic system, and it is compatible with any mode of life in the world, so long as the person pursuing that mode has embraced the orientation toward the spirit that our culture rejects.

Once we recognized that the monastic life we hoped to bring into being was a matter of an inner state of consciousness rather than an outward set of rules, the Hermitage of the Heart—the concept of living a monastic life of discipline and devotion in the midst of a confused and materialistic world—soon showed its possibilities. Since each individual's Awen is different, no one outward way of living in the world would be appropriate to more than a minority of participants in a new monasticism.

The issue of the central practice we meant to establish also involved a fair amount of discussion. Several of us had read an essay once fairly widely circulated in Neopagan circles, "A Mystery of Grain and Grape" by M.B. Wulf, which explored the idea that the Christian communion ritual could be repurposed for Neopagan use. Some of us had also participated in the communion ceremony of the Hermetic Order of the Golden Dawn, in which Osiris rather than Christ is invoked and rose, flame, bread, and wine are the elements of the communion. I also knew my way around the Sangreal Sodality communion ritual created by William G. Gray, the ceremonies of Dion Fortune's Guild of the Master Jesus, and a variety of other rituals of the same kind. That led me to begin experimenting with communion rituals suited to AODA's idiosyncratic practices, and in particular to its flexibility in terms of which if any deities a practitioner chooses to invoke.

The decision to use a ritual form with such close connections to the Christian tradition may seem either baffling or daring to those not familiar with AODA, but it was entirely in keeping with the traditions of the Druid Revival. As already noted, Druidry doesn't share the automatic hostility to Christianity found in so many other parts of the Neopagan scene, and the origins of the Universal Gnostic Church in Christian Universalism made any such hostility even more absurd in the context of the AODA.

For that matter, AODA had (and has) Christian Druid members. There were deeper issues as well. The Christian sacrament of Communion was itself modeled on older Pagan rituals in which foodstuffs were offered to deities and then consumed by the worshipers. Most traditional polytheist faiths have such ceremonies—in Hindu temples, for example, *prasad* (food offered to the gods) is reverently consumed by the faithful, and a visit to a Shinto shrine normally includes a sip of *sake* that has previously been offered to the *kami*. These age-old practices helped provide a context for our communion ritual.

With these points in mind, I set out to draft a ritual that could be practiced in the name and to the honor of any deity or deities, and that worked with the core spiritual energies of the AODA path—the solar and telluric currents, patterns of inner energy that descend from the sky and ascend from the earth to empower the religious and magical workings of the order. It took about a year to come up with something workable, but finally the ritual was tested by others and found entirely suitable. At that point we decided we were ready.

The Gnostic Celtic Church

As noted above, the Grand Grove had decided early on to create an independent organization for our monastic system. In 2010, after some discussion, we formally chartered the Gnostic Celtic Church (GCC) as that organization. More time went into setting up a simple structure for the leadership and a set of stages of ordination and consecration, and still more into coming up with a process of formation and screening for postulants to the GCC.

That was essential for a simple reason: the great majority of people who claim they want to learn and practice any spiritual system will never follow through on that claim. Among people who run correspondence courses in occultism and magic, it's a rule of thumb that at best, one student in twenty will actually do the work and finish the course. Many magical lodges thus make it standard practice to require prospective members to complete six months to a year of study by correspondence before they are admitted to lodge membership; the course is described, accurately if impolitely, as a "flake filter."

We knew from the beginning that we would need a "flake filter" for the GCC. Sure enough, once the rituals and requirements were published in early 2013 as *The Gnostic Celtic Church: A Manual and Book of Liturgy*, we got our share of flakes. Inevitably — despite detailed explanations of the church's purpose and mission on the order's email list and elsewhere — a majority of the first round of applicants wanted to become clergy so they could perform marriages, conduct services for paying congregations, and tell other people how to live their lives. Sara Greer, continuing her role as point person under the title of Presiding Archbishop of the GCC, adroitly handled most of these herself, but the other members of the Grand Grove got to hear about the more colorful stories. Fortunately, it wasn't too difficult to encourage people who were poorly suited to the guiding vision of the GCC to pursue their own Awen in some context better suited to their needs.

Growth was slow. We had intended all along that it should be so. It took a while for the first class of postulants to advance to the diaconate, and quite a bit longer for those first deacons to qualify for ordination to the GCC priesthood. By the time that process was well under way, I had stepped down as Grand Archdruid, settled into the less strenuous role of Archdruid Emeritus, and handed the reins of the order to a new Grand Archdruid, Gordon Cooper. Sara Greer stepped down three months before I did; a new Presiding Archbishop, Adam Robersmith, took charge of the GCC not long after, and slow but steady growth continues to this day.

That wasn't quite the end of my involvement with the GCC. Much of what followed, though, came through a channel I hadn't anticipated. The Grand Grove had decided early on to publish the GCC's rituals and practices in book form, and make the book available to the general public. We designed *The Gnostic Celtic Church: A Manual and Book of Liturgy* as a way to get around the common bad habit of making important rituals secret or insisting that only initiates of one sort or another could perform them. The GCC communion ritual, in fact, is designed so that anyone, irrespective of ordination or personal spiritual path, can perform it and get results. Ordination in the GCC confers not the right to perform the communion ritual but the obligation to do so regularly, and ordination is thus offered only to those whose personal Awen includes the regular performance of the rite. Getting the ritual into public circulation in book form was one way to put teeth in that decision, by guaranteeing that no one could ever try to monopolize access to it.

I didn't expect the concepts of the Rule of Awen and the Hermitage of the Heart to find an audience outside AODA. As several other essays in this volume demonstrate, though, that's what happened. Given the history of the GCC and the traditions that gave rise to it, this makes perfect sense. The enthusiastic Freemasons who founded AODA and the three Unitarian ministers who launched the UGC would doubtless have been astonished if they'd seen what unfolded from their creations; the elderly occultists who invited me to join AODA and then asked me to try to revive it certainly were startled by some of the ways it developed. The history of spirituality is anything but linear, after all. Awen, the spirit of inspiration, always adds its own influence to the mix, with results that nobody ever seems to be able to predict or entirely understand.

The Moral of the Story

This somewhat lengthy and labored explanation of the genesis of a modern monastic tradition within one Druid Revival organization hasn't been written for the sake of historical interest. The point I hope has been made by the slow and often uncertain process by which the Gnostic Celtic Church was born is that there is no one right way to create a monastic tradition—or, for that matter, a personal monastic vocation. Customs, practices, and ideas that are essential in the context of this or that historical example of monasticism can be optional, problematic, or dead wrong for a modern monasticism founded on different principles and unfolding from a different tradition. It can be necessary not merely to pick and choose, but to beg. borrow, steal, make things up, experiment, revise, and take risks, in order to craft something that will meet the needs of a given tradition and a given individual human being.

In a very real sense, the Hermitage of the Heart is a goal we strive toward, rather than a place we can inhabit. Which of us can honestly say that we can stand wholly apart from the pressures of our culture and our time, living lives of flawless discipline and devotion in response to our own unique inspiration and destiny? As a goal, though, it's worth striving for. If this essay helps anyone to pursue that quest, its purpose will be amply fulfilled.

About the Authors

Julie Bond, OSN, began her Druid studies in 1992 with the Order of Bards Ovates and Druids (OBOD). In 1996 she began developing a druidic monastic practice and in 2010 joined the Order of the Sacred Nemeton (OSN), a druid contemplative monastic order. She took her full vows with the OSN in 2012.

Patricia Christmas holds a BA in History from Lamar University and a MA in Anthropology from Texas State University-San Marcos, with a dual focus in archeology and iconography. She has practiced an eclectic form of polytheism, loosely based in Wicca, for 33 years. She has a daughter, son-in-law, and grandson of whom she is very proud. She began to feel the call towards an eremitic life more than a decade ago, and embraced the calling on Samhain in 2014. She currently lives in the greater Houston metro area with her sister, an assortment of cats, a small flock of chickens, and several thousand honeybees.

John Michael Greer is a widely read author, blogger, and astrologer whose work focuses on the overlaps between ecology, spirituality, and the future of industrial society. He served twelve years as Grand Archdruid of the Ancient Order of Druids in America, and remains active in that order as well as several other branches of Druid nature spirituality. He currently lives in East Providence, Rhode Island, with his wife Sara.

Kimberly Kirner is a cultural anthropologist, nature mystic, and animist Druid. She is a member of the Order of Bards, Ovates, and Druids (since 2005) and is one of the founders of the Star and Stone Druid Fellowship and the Grove of the Wild Wood Seed Group in Southern California. A professor of anthropology at California State University Northridge, her professional work centers on the relationships between cognition, emotion, and action and how these are shaped by place, community, and identity. As a Druid identifying with the goals and process of monastic life, she seeks to deepen her embodiment of ecocentric values in everyday life and her exploration of what it means to connect to the Divine through service to nature spirits and the Celtic gods through daily devotional practice.

Rebecca Korvo is a Gaelic and Heathen Polytheist, a member of the Ancient Order of Druids in America, and a devotee of Brigid, Who inspired her developing monastic practice. Under the name Rebecca Marjesdatter, she published a number of poems, won a Rhysling Award, served as poetry editor for the semiprozine "Tales of the Unanticipated," and was a member of the poetry performance group "Lady Poetesses from Hell." She lives in Minneapolis, Minnesota with her best friend, several cats, many shrines, and...no, there's no such thing as too many books.

Aine Llewellyn is a non-binary spirit worker who grew up in a Pagan household. They have been monastically-inclined since a teenager, when they first dedicated their life to their Gods and spirits. Their work primarily focuses on new (non-historic) spirits. They blog at https://www.patheos.com/blogs/ainellewellyn/

Janet Munin holds an MA in Comparative Religion from the University of Washington and has been spiritually-oriented for as long as she can remember. A hard polytheist, she venerates deities from the Northern and Ancient Near Eastern traditions. She is also the editor of *Queen of the Great Below: An Anthology In Honor of Ereshkigal*, published by Bibliotheca Alexandrina. In the course of working on this book, she has realized she is not called to monasticism at this time.

Syren Nagakyrie has been involved in pagan and polytheist communities for 20 years. They are the co-founder of a goddess temple, co-founder of the Alliance of Monastic Polytheist Pagans, and former organizer of a regional polytheist conference. They are now affiliated with a Shakta Tantra tradition within Hinduism. Syren has been developing a monastic life for the past five years.

Danica Swanson is a writer, editor, music journalist, incubation space designer, and contemplative animist-polytheist. In service to Skaði and other Ásynjur since 2004, Danica founded Black Stone Sanctuary, an incubation retreat inspired by the pre-Christian religious and folk traditions of her Swedish and German ancestral lineage. Her community service work includes three years as a founder, admin, and online community manager for polytheistic monastic discussion forums.

PAGANISM & SHAMANISM

What is Paganism? A religion, a spirituality, an alternative belief system, nature worship? You can find support for all these definitions (and many more) in dictionaries, encyclopaedias, and text books of religion, but subscribe to any one and the truth will evade you. Above all Paganism is a creative pursuit, an encounter with reality, an exploration of meaning and an expression of the soul. Druids, Heathens, Wiccans and others, all contribute their insights and literary riches to the Pagan tradition. Moon Books invites you to begin or to deepen your own encounter, right here, right now.

If you have enjoyed this book, why not tell other readers by posting a review on your preferred book site.

Medicine for the Soul
The Complete Book of Shamanic Healing
Ross Heaven
All you will ever need to know about shamanic healing and how to become your own shaman...
Paperback: 978-1-78099-419-2 ebook: 978-1-78099-420-8

Shaman Pathways – The Druid Shaman
Exploring the Celtic Otherworld
Danu Forest
A practical guide to Celtic shamanism with exercises and techniques as well as traditional lore for exploring the Celtic Otherworld.
Paperback: 978-1-78099-615-8 ebook: 978-1-78099-616-5

Traditional Witchcraft for the Woods and Forests
A Witch's Guide to the Woodland with Guided Meditations and Pathworking
Melusine Draco
A Witch's guide to walking alone in the woods, with guided meditations and pathworking.
Paperback: 978-1-84694-803-9 ebook: 978-1-84694-804-6

Wild Earth, Wild Soul
A Manual for an Ecstatic Culture
Bill Pfeiffer
Imagine a nature-based culture so alive and so connected, spreading like wildfire. This book is the first flame...
Paperback: 978-1-78099-187-0 ebook: 978-1-78099-188-7

Naming the Goddess
Trevor Greenfield
Naming the Goddess is written by over eighty adherents and
scholars of Goddess and Goddess Spirituality.
Paperback: 978-1-78279-476-9 ebook: 978-1-78279-475-2

Shapeshifting into Higher Consciousness
Heal and Transform Yourself and Our World with Ancient
Shamanic and Modern Methods
Llyn Roberts
Ancient and modern methods that you can use every day to
transform yourself and make a positive difference in the world.
Paperback: 978-1-84694-843-5 ebook: 978-1-84694-844-2

Readers of ebooks can buy or view any of these bestsellers by
clicking on the live link in the title. Most titles are published in
paperback and as an ebook. Paperbacks are available in traditional
bookshops. Both print and ebook formats are available online.

Find more titles and sign up to our readers' newsletter at
http://www.johnhuntpublishing.com/paganism
Follow us on Facebook at https://www.facebook.com/MoonBooks
and Twitter at https://twitter.com/MoonBooksJHP